COOKING
OF THE
American
South

George Kerhulas

**CHARTWELL
BOOKS, INC.**

This book is dedicated to Edward and
Doris Hylen.

Special thanks to Tony Meisel and
Sheila Buff.

Copyright © 1985 Footnote
Productions Ltd.

ISBN: 0–89009–956–1

Typeset by CST, Eastbourne, England.
Color separations in Hongkong
Manufactured by Regent Publishing
Services Limited.

This book was designed and produced
by Footnote Productions Ltd.
6 Blundell Street, London, N7

Printed in Hong Kong.

CHARTWELL BOOKS, INC.
A Division of
BOOK SALES, INC.
110 Enterprise Avenue
Secaucus, New Jersey 07094

CONTENTS

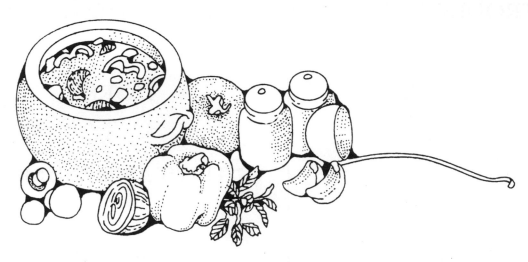

INTRODUCTION

The popular image of the American South promulgated by books and movies is one of plantation houses, cotton fields, gracious manners and stern honor. This may have been true once upon a time and for a small minority, but it certainly is a fantasy vision applied to a vast sweep of country. In truth, many Southlands exist, each with its own special character and customs and its unique culinary traditions.

The first Southern gourmet was undoubtedly Thomas Jefferson, not only a statesman, educator, architect and writer, but also an experimental farmer and cultivator of the palate extra-

ordinaire. We know that the gentry ate well and with elegance. Great feasts of game and local hams, elaborate sweets (George Washington had an ice cream machine), fanciful salads and seafood attest to the bounty available to the original settlers as well as their concern for keeping a good table. Wines in abundance and variety were imported. New breeds of animals and new species of fruits and vegetables were imported and cross-bred with native American varieties.

This tradition of good eating never left the South, but it appears differently in various locales. From the seafood of Tidewater Virginia to the peanut-fed hogs of the Deep South to the stone crabs and key limes of Florida and the grits of Mississippi to the gumbos and jambalayas of Louisiana, the one thing all these areas have in common is abundance, graciousness and simplicity.

Each "South" has, of course, been influenced by many factors: geography, economic development, local resources and trade. This last left an indelible imprint through the importation of slaves from Africa and the West Indies. These slaves brought their local traditions and cooking with them, adapted them to locally available ingredients, and permanently infused American cooking with a unique character. The gumbos of Louisiana's bayou country are direct descendants of West Indian slave cooking. The many variations on rice and beans or peas also derive from African slave dishes. Dishes using sesame seeds, or benne, are also a legacy of African slaves, who brought the seeds to America. The list can go on and on.

As noted, the South is many things to many people. In COOKING OF THE AMERICAN SOUTH you will find dishes from every Southern state. Crab cakes from Maryland. Baked hams from Virginia. Burgoo from Kentucky. Key lime pie from Florida. She-crab soup from South Carolina. Hush puppies and corn pone from Georgia. Gumbos from Louisiana. Chitlins from Mississippi. Breads and cakes and pies and puddings from all over.

Southern cooking is a vast cornucopia of substantial and delicate, spicy and bland, hot and cool foods, each with its own special contribution to the savor of the South. They will add variety and, one hopes, graciousness to your table and tempt your family with the flavors of one of our oldest culinary traditions.

APPETIZERS

BAKED AVOCADOS STUFFED WITH CRAB

serves 6

3 large ripe avocados
6 teaspoons lemon juice
1½ cups crabmeat, flaked
1 cup milk
1 onion slice, finely chopped
½ teaspoon chopped parsley
2 tablespoons butter, melted
2 tablespoons flour
2 tablespoons heavy cream
½ teaspoon salt
½ teaspoon white pepper
½ teaspoon nutmeg
¼ teaspoon hot red-pepper sauce
1 tablespoon drained capers
6 tablespoons grated mild cheese

●

Preheat the oven to 350°F. Slice the avocados in half lengthwise and remove the pits. Place the halves, skin-side down, in a shallow baking pan with ½ inch of water. Sprinkle each avocado half with 1 teaspoon lemon juice.

Combine the crabmeat, milk, onion, parsley, butter, flour, cream, salt, pepper, nutmeg, hot red-pepper sauce and capers in a saucepan. Cook over medium heat, stirring constantly, until thick. Spoon the crab mixture into the avocados and cook for 15 minutes. Remove from the oven and sprinkle each avocado half with 1 tablespoon of cheese. Cook for 10 minutes more and cool slightly before serving.

CHEESE STRAWS

serves 6 to 8

1 cup grated Parmesan cheese
1 cup flour
salt to taste
cayenne pepper to taste
1 tablespoon melted butter
1 egg yolk, beaten

●

Preheat the oven to 450°F.

Combine the flour and cheese in a mixing bowl. Add the salt and cayenne. Add the beaten egg yolk and the melted butter. Mix gently to form a paste.

Roll the dough out onto a lightly floured surface to ⅛-inch thickness. With a pastry wheel or sharp knife, cut the dough into strips 4 inches long. Place the strips on heavily greased baking sheets and bake until light brown, about 5 to 7 minutes. Cool slightly and remove from sheets.

CHOW-CHOW

makes 7 quarts

9 green tomatoes, chopped
8 large onions, chopped
10 green bell peppers, chopped
4 small hot red peppers, chopped
3 tablespoons salt
1 quart white vinegar
2 cinnamon sticks
½ teaspoon whole cloves
3 tablespoons dry mustard
2 bay leaves
2 cups sugar
½ cup grated horseradish

•

Combine the tomatoes, onions, bell peppers and hot red peppers in a large bowl and cover with the salt. Cover the bowl and refrigerate overnight.

Drain any liquid that has formed in the bowl and transfer the vegetables to a large pot. Add the vinegar to the pot. Tie the cinnamon, cloves, mustard, and bay leaves together in a piece of cheesecloth and add to the pot. Stir in the sugar and horseradish and bring to a boil, stirring constantly. Reduce heat and simmer for 15 minutes.

Pour the mixture into sterilized jars that have tight-fitting lids and refrigerate. Serve with assortment of breads, crackers and fresh vegetables.

CORN AND PEPPER SALAD

makes about 3 quarts

24 ears fresh corn
1 medium-sized head cabbage
2 onions
3 green bell peppers
3 red bell peppers
2 cups sugar
2 tablespoons salt
3 tablespoons mustard seeds
5 cups distilled white vinegar

•

Cut the corn from the cobs with a sharp knife.

Finely chop the cabbage, onions, green bell peppers, and red bell peppers.

Place the corn and chopped vegetables into a large saucepan. Add the sugar, salt, mustard seeds and vinegar. Bring to a boil. Reduce the heat and simmer for 20 minutes.

Remove from the heat and spoon the relish into hot sterilized jars. Seal, cool and store.

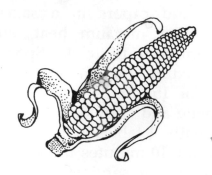

CRAB DIP

makes 3 cups

6 ounces cream cheese, softened
2 tablespoons very finely chopped onion
1 teaspoon Worcestershire sauce
1 teaspoon hot red-pepper sauce
salt to taste
black pepper to taste
4 tablespoons mayonnaise
1 pound cooked crabmeat, flaked

•

In a bowl combine the cream cheese, onion, Worcestershire sauce, hot red-pepper sauce, salt, pepper and mayonnaise. Mix well. Add the crabmeat and mix again.

CRABMEAT SPREAD

makes 2 cups

1 cup sour cream
1 teaspoon curry powder
1 tablespoon finely chopped onion
¼ teaspoon black pepper
salt to taste
½ cup unsweetened shredded coconut
¼ pound cooked crabmeat, flaked

•

In a bowl combine the sour cream, curry, onion, pepper, salt and coconut. Mix well. Add the crabmeat and mix again.

CREOLE CANAPÉS

serves 6

1 cup finely minced boiled ham
1 medium white onion, finely minced
2 garlic cloves, finely minced
1 medium tomato, cored, peeled and finely chopped
1 large jalapeño pepper, stemmed, seeded and finely chopped
½ teaspoon salt
1 teaspoon cayenne pepper
⅛ teaspoon hot red-pepper sauce
1 tablespoon butter
2 ounces softened cream cheese
6 slices pumpernickel bread, toasted, buttered and cut into strips
1 teaspoon paprika

•

Combine the ham, onion, garlic, tomato, jalapeño pepper, salt, pepper, hot red-pepper sauce and butter in a skillet and sauté over medium-low heat for 7 minutes. Allow the mixture to cool for 30 minutes.

Preheat the oven to 375°F.

Combine the ham mixture with the cream cheese and blend thoroughly. Spread the mixture onto the toast strips and arrange on a cookie sheet. Sprinkle with paprika and bake for 6 minutes. Serve hot.

CRAB PUFFS

serves 6

1 cup sifted flour
½ teaspoon salt
½ teaspoon black pepper
1 cup beer
8 tablespoons butter
2 eggs
½ pound cooked crabmeat, flaked

•

Preheat the oven to 450°F. In a mixing bowl, combine the flour, salt and pepper and set aside.

Place the beer in a saucepan and bring to a slow boil. When the beer begins to simmer stir in the butter. Continue to stir until the butter is well blended with the beer.

When the mixture begins to boil, reduce the heat to low and stir in the flour mixture until well blended. Cook over low heat until the mixture begins to pull away from the sides of the saucepan. Remove the saucepan from the heat and beat in the eggs, one at a time.

Lightly grease a large cookie sheet. Drop the dough by heaping teaspoons onto the cookie sheet, 1 inch apart. Place the cookie sheet on the top rack of the oven and bake for 10 minutes. Reduce the heat to 350°F and cook for 5 minutes more.

Remove the cookie sheet carefully from the oven and set it on a flat surface. With a sharp knife, split the tops of the puffs and spoon in the crabmeat.

Place the cookie sheet back into the oven and bake for 5 minutes more, or until the puffs are golden brown. Allow the puffs to cool slightly before serving. Serve with Tabasco or Worcestershire sauce.

CRY BABIES

serves 6

2 cups sifted flour
½ cup sugar
½ cup lard or solid white shortening, softened
1 egg, beaten
½ cup dark molasses
½ tablespoon ground ginger
½ teaspoon salt
⅔ cup boiling water
½ tablespoon baking soda

•

Preheat the oven to 350°F.

Blend all the ingredients together in a large mixing bowl and mix until stiff. (Add more flour if not stiff.)

Drop the batter by spoonfuls onto a greased cookie sheet. Bake for 6 minutes or until golden in color. Cool slightly before serving.

DEEP-FRIED HAM FRITTERS

serves 15

1 pound baked Virginia ham
½ cup unsweetened crushed
pineapple, drained
¾ cup white flour
1 teaspoon baking powder
¼ cup light cream
¼ cup cold water
1 teaspoon Angostura or Peychand's
bitters
1 teaspoon sherry
2 eggs
oil for deep frying

•

Mince or grind the ham until it is like coarse meal. Mix the pineapple together with the ham in a bowl.

Sift the flour and baking powder together in a mixing bowl. Add the cream, water, bitters, sherry and eggs and beat until the mixture is smooth. Fold in the ham and pineapple mixture and mix together with a wooden spoon until well blended.

Set the bowl in the freezer for about 15 minutes.

Heat the oil in a deep fryer until it is no hotter than 350°F.

Drop large spoonfuls of the fritter mixture, using a spatula to scrape the spoonfuls into the deep-fryer. Cook until the fritters are golden brown. Drain on paper towels and serve hot with apple sauce or spicy mustard.

DEVILED EGGS

makes 20

10 hard-cooked eggs
5 tablespoons mayonnaise
3 teaspoons French-style mustard
2 teaspoons vinegar
2 teaspoons lemon juice
½ teaspoon salt
½ teaspoon white pepper
1 teaspoon paprika

•

Carefully slice the eggs in half lengthwise. Remove the yolks and put them in a mixing bowl. Mash the yolks with a fork and blend in the mayonnaise, mustard, vinegar, lemon juice, salt and white pepper. When a smooth paste is formed, spoon back into the white halves and sprinkle with paprika. Refrigerate for 30 minutes before serving.

DEVILED EGGS WITH ANCHOVIES

serves 6

6 large, hard-cooked eggs
1 teaspoon French-style mustard
¼ teaspoon chopped parsley
½ teaspoon salt
1 tablespoon lemon juice
1 tablespoon olive oil
1 tablespoon capers, well drained and finely chopped
1 teaspoon mayonnaise
6 rolled anchovies (optional)
1 teaspoon paprika

•

Carefully slice the eggs in half lengthwise and put the yolks in a mixing bowl. Place the egg halves on a bed of crisp lettuce and place in the refrigerator.

With a fork, mash the yolks and blend in the mustard, parsley, salt, lemon juice, olive oil, capers and mayonnaise. Blend the mixture well.

Slice the anchovies in half through the middle with a sharp knife, so as to keep the round shape of each half.

Remove the eggs from the refrigerator and fill them with an equal portion of the yolk mix.

Place one half anchovy roll on each egg and sprinkle with paprika before serving.

EGGPLANT CAVIAR

serves 6

1 large eggplant
1 large onion, finely chopped
1 green bell pepper, finely chopped
½ cup olive oil
2 garlic cloves, minced
2 tomatoes, peeled, seeded and chopped
½ teaspoon salt
½ teaspoon cayenne pepper
4 tablespoons dry vermouth

•

Preheat the oven to 400°F. Place the whole eggplant in a lightly oiled baking dish and bake for 1 hour. Remove from the oven and allow to cool. When the eggplant is cool enough to handle, peel it and finely chop the meat. Set aside.

Place the onion, bell pepper, olive oil and garlic in a large skillet and sauté over medium-low heat. Do not brown.

Add the eggplant, tomatoes, salt, cayenne pepper and vermouth and stir gently over low heat. Allow to cook for 25 minutes, stirring occasionally, until the mixture is thick. Transfer the mixture to a serving dish and refrigerate overnight. Serve with bread or an assortment of crackers.

DEVILISH OYSTERS

serves 6

3 tablespoons dry mustard
36 oysters, shelled, rinsed and drained
2 eggs, beaten
1 cup unflavored breadcrumbs
1 cup cracker meal
6 tablespoons melted butter

•

In a saucepan, combine the dry mustard with a little water to form a smooth paste, and gently stir in the oysters. Cook over low heat for 2 minutes. Remove the pan from the stove and allow the oysters to cool. Oysters should be thoroughly coated.

Beat the 2 eggs in one bowl and combine the breadcrumbs and cracker meal in another. Preheat the broiler.

When the oysters are cool, dip each one in the egg and then gently roll in the crumb mixture. Place the breaded oysters in a well-buttered baking pan.

Sprinkle the oysters with melted butter and broil quickly to brown both sides. Serve with lemon wedges.

GREEN TOMATO RELISH

makes about 2 to 2½ pints

4 to 5 pounds green tomatoes, chopped
2 medium-sized onions, chopped
2 quarts cold water
½ cup salt
1½ cups white vinegar
½ cup boiling water
1½ cups sugar
1½ teaspoons celery seeds
½ teaspoon cinnamon
½ teaspoon ground turmeric
¼ teaspoon dry mustard

•

Place the tomatoes and onions in a large bowl. Pour the cold water over them and sprinkle with the salt. Soak for 3 hours.

Drain the tomatoes and onions in a colander. Rinse well with cold water.

In a saucepan combine the vinegar, boiling water, sugar, celery seeds, cinnamon, turmeric and mustard. Bring the mixture to a boil and boil for 3 minutes. Add the tomatoes and onions and bring to a boil again. Lower the heat and simmer, uncovered, for 10 minutes. Remove from heat.

Carefully spoon the relish into hot sterilized jars. Seal, cool, and store.

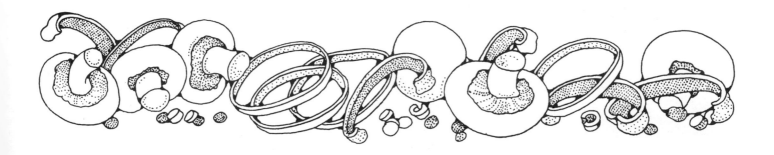

GUACAMOLE

serves 6

2 large ripe avocados
1 large tomato, peeled, seeded, and
finely chopped
1 hard-cooked egg, finely chopped
1 medium onion, finely chopped
2 whole green chilies, stemmed,
seeded, and finely chopped
1 tablespoon lemon juice
1 teaspoon salt
½ teaspoon cumin
½ teaspoon cayenne pepper
¼ teaspoon hot red-pepper sauce

•

Cut the avocados in half and remove the pits. Scoop out the flesh with a spoon and place it in a large mixing bowl. Mash well with a fork. Add all of the remaining ingredients. Blend well, cover and refrigerate for 1 hour before seving with cornchips.

HOMINY BALLS

serves 6

2 cups water
1 teaspoon salt
½ cup quick-cooking hominy grits
1 cup sharp cheddar cheese, grated
½ teaspoon cayenne pepper
¼ teaspoon nutmeg
2 eggs
1½ teaspoons olive oil
1 cup fine unflavored breadcrumbs
½ cup cracker meal
vegetable oil for frying

•

Combine the water and salt in a saucepan and bring to a boil. Slowly add the grits, stirring constantly. Bring the mixture back to a boil, reduce heat and cook for 5 minutes, stirring occasionally. Remove from heat and chill.

Place the chilled grits in a large mixing bowl and add the cheese, pepper and nutmeg. Mash the ingredients in the bowl until well blended. Use a melon baller to scoop the mixture into balls. Place on a plate and set aside.

Put a skillet filled with vegetable oil to a depth of ½-inch over medium heat.

While waiting for the oil to heat, combine the eggs and olive oil in a bowl and beat well. Combine the breadcrumbs and cracker meal together in a shallow bowl.

When the oil is hot, dip the balls into the egg then roll in the crumb mixture and carefully drop into the oil. Cook each ball for 1 minute, roll over to other side and cook for 1 minute more. Drain on paper towels before serving. Serve with an assortment of sauces.

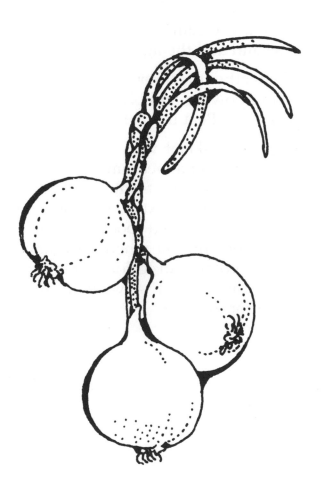

MUSHROOMS STUFFED WITH CREAM CHEESE

serves 6

**1 pound large mushrooms
2 teaspoons Worcestershire sauce
½ teaspoon paprika
1 tablespoon lemon juice
1 teaspoon chopped parsley
2 anchovy fillets, drained and finely minced
2 ounces cream cheese, softened
¼ cup sour cream**

•

Remove the stems from the mushrooms and wash and drain the caps. Cut off and discard the hard ends of the stems. Rinse, drain and finely chop the stems.

Combine the chopped stems, Worcestershire sauce, paprika, lemon juice, parsley and anchovies in a mixing bowl and let stand for 10 minutes.

In a separate bowl combine the cream cheese and sour cream and mix until well blended. Add the stem mixture to the cheese mixture and mix well.

Fill each mushroom cap with an equal portion of the cheese mixture and refrigerate for at least one hour before serving.

LIME RELISH

makes 2 pints

12 limes, washed
cold water
1½ cups sugar
1 cup vinegar
½ cup water

•

Place the limes in a large pot and add enough cold water to cover. Soak the limes for 24 hours.

Drain the limes and return them to the pot. Add enough cold water to cover and cook for 15 to 20 minutes, or until limes can be easily pierced with a fork. Drain well and set aside to cool.

When the limes are cool, cut them into eighths. Remove the seeds. Set the limes aside.

Place the sugar, vinegar and water in a saucepan. Cook over medium-low heat until syrupy, about 15 minutes.

Place the lime pieces into hot sterilized jars. Cover with the syrup. Seal, cool, and store.

ORANGE CRITTERS

serves 6

1 cup light cream
1 egg, beaten lightly
1 cup sifted flour
1 teaspoon cinnamon
1 teaspoon baking powder
vegetable oil for frying
3 large oranges, peeled, seeded and broken into sections

•

Place the cream in a large mixing bowl and add the lightly beaten egg.

Sift together the flour, cinnamon and baking powder and blend them into the cream. Beat until almost stiff.

Fill a deep skillet with 1 inch of oil and place over a medium heat. Drop the orange segments into the batter, then spoon the mixture out into the hot oil. Use a slotted spoon to remove them from the oil when they have turned golden in color. Drain on paper towels and serve with sour cream for dipping.

PARTY PECANS

makes 4 cups

2 tablespoons peanut oil
½ cup Worcestershire sauce
1 tablespoon mild barbecue sauce
¼ teaspoon hot red-pepper sauce
4 cups pecan halves
salt to taste
black pepper to taste

•

Pour the peanut oil, Worcestershire sauce, barbecue sauce and hot red-pepper sauce into a mixing bowl and stir. Stir in the pecans.

Preheat the oven to 300°F.

Line a baking pan with aluminum foil and spread the pecans and sauce evenly on it. Bake for 30 minutes stirring every 7 minutes. Drain the roasted pecans on brown paper. Season with salt and pepper to taste.

SMOKED SALMON CANAPÉS

serves 6

8 ounces smoked salmon, thinly sliced
2 tablespoons sweet butter, softened
1 teaspoon drained prepared white horseradish
1 tablespoon finely chopped parsley
¼ teaspoon hot red-pepper sauce
8 thin slices of pumpernickel bread
64 capers, drained

•

In a small mixing bowl combine the butter, horseradish, parsley and hot red-pepper sauce. Spread a thin layer of the mixture on each slice of bread.

Cover each slice of bread with a single layer of the smoked salmon. Cut each slice of bread into quarters. Garnish each bread square with two capers and serve.

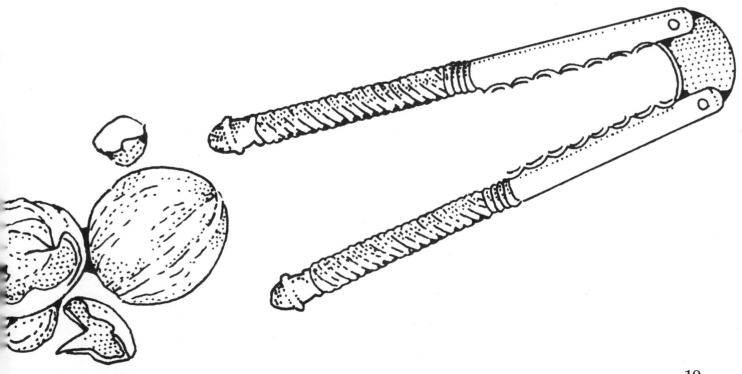

SWEET PICKLED PEACHES

makes 3 quarts

6 pounds firm fresh peaches
3 cups cider vinegar
3 cups sugar
½ teaspoon whole cloves
½ teaspoon allspice
½ teaspoon nutmeg
1 teaspoon cinnamon

•

Place the peaches in a large mixing bowl and pour enough boiling water over them to cover. Allow the peaches to remain in the hot water for 7 minutes. Remove from the water and drain. Carefully peel the skin off the peaches. Slice them in half and remove the pits. Divide the peach halves among three sterilized 1-quart jars, cover and refrigerate.

Combine the vinegar and sugar in a large saucepan and bring to a boil. Add the remaining ingredients and continue to boil for 5 minutes.

Remove the peaches from the refrigerator and take off the caps. When the liquid is ready, divide it among the three jars. Re-cap the jars and return to the refrigerator for at least 24 hours before serving.

SMOKED TROUT MOUSSE

serves 8

12 ounces smoked trout (no skin or bones)
1 scallion, chopped
½ teaspoon white pepper
¼ teaspoon nutmeg
2 teaspoons chopped fresh dill
1 package unflavored gelatin
1½ cups heavy cream
½ cup plain yogurt

•

Break the trout up into pieces and place into a blender or food processor with the scallion, pepper, nutmeg and dill. Blend into a purée. (Add a little water if necessary.)

Put the cream in a saucepan with the gelatin, and stir over a low heat until the gelatin dissolves.

Add the cream mixture and the yogurt to the trout mixture in the blender and blend until smooth. Pour into a 3-cup mold and refrigerate overnight.

To unmold, run a knife around the edge and then hold the mold in a pan of hot water, shaking gently, until the mousse has pulled away from the mold. Unmold on a serving dish, garnish and serve.

SOUPS

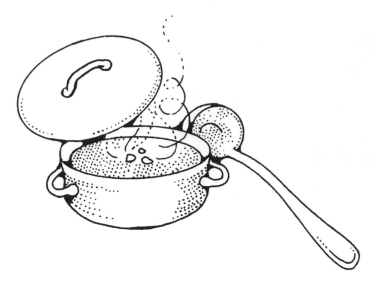

ALMOND CHICKEN SOUP

serves 6

½ cup blanched almonds, finely
chopped
3 cups chicken broth
1 teaspoon onion juice
1 bay leaf, finely crushed
3 tablespoons sifted flour
3 tablespoons butter
2 cups milk
1 cup half-and-half or light cream
½ teaspoon salt
½ teaspoon black pepper

•

Place the almonds in a large saucepan
and add the chicken broth, onion
juice and bay leaf. Simmer for
15 minutes. Sprinkle in the flour and
stir in the butter until well blended.
Stir in the milk, half-and-half, salt
and pepper and blend well. Simmer
for 5 more minutes and serve.

BLACK-EYED PEA SOUP

serves 6

2 cups dried black-eyed peas
1 large hambone with meat or 1 large
hamhock
2 medium onions, chopped
2 chopped carrots
3 stalks chopped celery
5 sprigs chopped parsley
3 whole cloves
¼ teaspoon allspice
¼ teaspoon thyme
2 bay leaves
1 teaspoon dry mustard
1 tablespoon Worcestershire sauce
¼ cup dry sherry
2 hard-cooked eggs, thinly sliced
1 lemon, thinly sliced

•

Soak the peas overnight in enough
cold water to cover them to a depth
of 1 inch.

Drain the peas and place them in a
large cooking pot with 8 cups water,
the hambone, onion, carrots, celery,
parsley, cloves, allspice, thyme, bay
leaves, mustard and Worcestershire
sauce.

Bring to a boil and lower the heat.
Cook for 3 hours, covered. Remove
the hambone, cutting any meat into
small pieces, and putting them back
into the soup.

Stir in the sherry then gently float in
the egg and the lemon slices. Serve.

CARROT SOUP

serves 6

4 large carrots, finely chopped
2 large onions, finely chopped
1 turnip, peeled and finely chopped
2 celery stalks, finely chopped
2 cloves
½ teaspoon thyme
6 cups cold water
8 cups boiling water
1 teaspoon cornstarch
4 cups milk
1 teaspoon salt
1 teaspoon black pepper

•

Place the carrots, onions, turnip, celery, cloves, and thyme in a large pot and add the cold water.

Bring to a boil and lower the heat. Simmer for 25 minutes. Remove the cloves, drain off and discard the water and mash the vegetables through a large sieve back into the cooking pot. Add the boiling water, cover and simmer over low heat for 15 minutes.

Mix the cornstarch with one tablespoon of the milk and add it to the soup after the first 5 minutes of simmering time. Combine the remaining milk and the salt and pepper in a large skillet and heat over medium heat almost to a boil.

Add the milk mixture to the soup, stirring gently, and simmer for 5 minutes more. Serve hot.

CATFISH SOUP

serves 6

3 pounds catfish, boned, skinned and cut into pieces
¼ pound bacon
1 small onion, chopped
1 tablespoon chopped parsley
½ teaspoon salt
1 teaspoon black pepper
4 cups water
2 tablespoons butter
1 tablespoon flour
1 cup hot milk
2 egg yolks, slightly beaten

•

In a large pot, combine the catfish, bacon, onion, parsley, salt, pepper and water. Simmer over medium heat until the fish is cooked, but not yet falling apart.

Discard the bacon, then lift out the fish with a slotted spoon and place in a large soup tureen.

Melt the butter in a small saucepan and blend in the flour. Stir well and blend in the milk. Stir until it begins to thicken, then stir the milk mixture into the soup.

Bring the soup back to a simmer, remove from heat, stir in the egg yolks and pour the soup over the catfish. Serve at once.

CELERY CHOWDER

serves 4

1 medium onion, chopped
2 tablespoons butter
4 cups finely diced celery
3 large potatoes, peeled and finely
diced
1 teaspoon salt
1 teaspoon black pepper
1 quart light cream
2 tablespoons sifted flour
2 hard-cooked eggs, crumbled

•

In a large skillet sauté the onion in the butter until soft. Stir in the celery and continue to sauté until the celery is soft. Stir in the potatoes and stir untill all the ingredients are light golden in color. Cover with boiling water and simmer for 15 minutes.

Add the salt, pepper and light cream, stir well and bring almost to a boil. Sprinkle the flour in and blend well, lowering the heat. Simmer for 5 minutes, stirring constantly. Add the eggs and serve.

COLD CURRY SOUP

serves 4

3 tablespoons butter
2 tablespoons curry powder
4 cups chicken broth
6 egg yolks, lightly beaten
½ cup light cream
½ cup heavy cream
1 tablespoon fresh chopped parsley

•

Place the butter in a large saucepan and melt over medium heat. Sprinkle the curry powder over the melting butter and stir until well blended. Simmer for 2 minutes.

Stir in the broth and bring the mixture to a boil. When the soup begins to boil, lower the heat and whisk in first the yolks, and then the light and heavy cream.

Stir constantly over low heat until the soup begins to thicken. Do not let the soup come back to a boil.

Pour the soup into a large serving bowl and sprinkle it with the chopped parsley. Cover and refrigerate for 4 hours before serving.

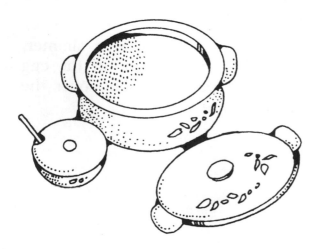

CORN CHOWDER

serves 4

2 cups fresh corn
¼ pound bacon, diced
1 onion, sliced and broken into rings
2 cups diced peeled potatoes
½ teaspoon salt
¼ teaspoon black pepper
boiling water
½ cup milk
4 milk crackers

•

Place the bacon in a large skillet and cook until medium-well done. While waiting for the bacon to cook, arrange the corn and potatoes in layers in a large pot.

Add the onion to the bacon and cook until tender.

Remove the bacon and onion and set aside.

Pour the bacon drippings over the corn and potatoes and then cover them with the bacon and onion. Add the salt and pepper. Pour in enough boiling water to cover the food to a depth of 1 inch. Bring to a boil, lower the heat and simmer, covered, for 1 hour.

Before serving, place the milk crackers in a large serving dish and cover with the milk. When the soup is ready, pour it over the milk and blend well.

COLD BUTTERMILK SOUP

serves 4

1 quart buttermilk
½ large cucumber, peeled and finely diced
½ cup cooked shrimp, peeled and deveined
1 small tomato, peeled and finely diced
1 teaspoon dried dill or 3 teaspoons chopped fresh dill
1 teaspoon chopped parsley

•

Combine the buttermilk and cucumber in a blender and blend on low for 1 minute.

Add the shrimp and tomato and blend on low for 30 seconds. Pour the mixture into a serving bowl and cover. Refrigerate for at least 2 hours.

Stir in the dill and sprinkle with the parsley before serving.

CORN AND SHRIMP CHOWDER

serves 8

3 tablespoons butter
¼ cup chopped scallions
1 garlic clove, finely minced
¼ teaspoon black pepper
1½ cups light cream
½ cup water
2 potatoes, peeled and diced
¼ teaspoon salt
½ teaspoon dried parsley
2 cups milk
3 ounces cream cheese
1 cup whole kernel corn, drained
1½ pounds fresh shrimp, shelled,
deveined and chopped

•

Melt the butter in a large heavy pot or Dutch oven. Add the scallions, garlic and pepper and sauté over low heat until the scallions are tender but not browned.

Add the cream, water, potatoes, salt, parsley and milk. Simmer for 15 to 20 minutes, or until the potatoes are soft. Stir frequently so the cream and milk do not form a skin. Do not allow the mixture to come to a boil.

Soften the cream cheese with a fork, then stir it into the soup. When the cream cheese is fully blended, add the corn and shrimp. Bring the soup slowly to a boil, then immediately reduce the heat and simmer for 5 to 10 minutes, or until the shrimp are white and tender. Serve the chowder piping hot.

CREOLE SALPICON

serves 6

3 tablespoons butter
3 tablespoons sifted flour
2 cups boiling milk
1 teaspoon grated nutmeg
½ teaspoon salt
2 teaspoons cayenne pepper
1 teaspoon oregano
1 herb bouquet (1 bay leaf, 12
peppercorns, 4 cloves, 2 sprigs of
parsley, tied in a cheesecloth)
meat from 24 crawfish, finely chopped
3 tomatoes, peeled and finely chopped
1 dozen mushrooms, minced

•

Melt the butter in a large saucepan and sprinkle with the flour. Cook for 5 minutes, stirring constantly.

Gradually whisk in the boiling milk, and add the nutmeg, salt, cayenne pepper, oregano and herb bouquet. Continue to cook over medium heat for 15 minutes, stirring often.

Discard the herb bouquet and gently stir in the crawfish, tomatoes and mushrooms. Continue cooking over medium heat for 5 minutes more and serve.

CREAM OF PEANUT SOUP

serves 8

1 medium onion, finely chopped
2 celery stalks, finely chopped
1 tablespoon flour
5 tablespoons butter
1 tablespoon flour
1 cup smooth peanut butter
2 cups light cream
½ teaspoon salt
½ teaspoon black pepper
¼ cup chopped unsalted peanuts

•

In a large skillet, sauté the onion and celery in the butter until soft, but not brown. Add the flour and blend well. Pour in 1 cup of the chicken broth and stir constantly while bringing the mixture to a boil.

Remove the mixture from the heat and allow to cool slightly. Pour it into a blender and blend on low for 1 minute. Put the blended mixture into a large pot and add the remaining chicken broth.

While the mixture heats over low heat, whisk in the cream and peanut butter. Blend well.

As the soup is thickening, blend in the salt and pepper. Sprinkle with the chopped peanuts and serve.

CREAM OF TURKEY SOUP

serves 6

½ cup butter
6 tablespoons sifted flour
1 teaspoon salt
½ teaspoon black pepper
2 cups light cream
3 cups turkey or chicken broth
1 cup coarsely chopped cooked turkey

•

Melt the butter in a large saucepan and blend in the flour, salt and pepper. Heat until the mixture begins to bubble.

Gradually stir in the cream and 1 cup of the broth. Stirring constantly, bring to a boil for 1 minute, then reduce the heat. Blend in remaining broth and the turkey. Simmer for 10 minutes and serve.

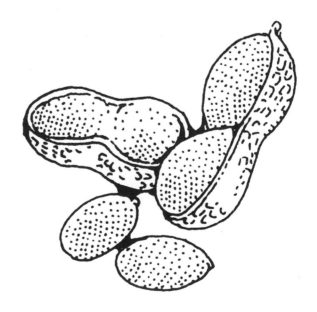

CREOLE BOUILLABAISSE

serves 6

1 pound red snapper fillets, sliced into
large pieces
1 pound redfish fillets, sliced into large
pieces
2 teaspoons minced parsley
1 teaspoon salt
¾ teaspoon thyme
½ teaspoon allspice
¼ teaspoon black pepper
2 bay leaves, finely crushed
1 garlic clove, finely minced
3 tablespoons olive oil
1 large onion, chopped
1 cup white wine
3 large ripe tomatoes, peeled and
chopped
1 lemon, thinly sliced
1 cup hot fish stock or hot water
1 teaspoon salt
½ teaspoon black pepper
½ teaspoon cayenne pepper
1 teaspoon hot red-pepper sauce
¼ teaspoon saffron
6 thick slices buttered toast

•

Place the fillets on a platter. Mix the parsley, salt, thyme, allspice, pepper, bay leaves and garlic in a bowl. Rub the mixture into the fillets and set aside.

Heat the olive oil in a large saucepan and stir in the onion; sauté until tender. Add the fillets and brown on both sides, for 5 minutes. Remove the fillets to the platter and place in the oven to keep warm.

Stir the wine into the pan and blend in the tomatoes. Bring to a boil. Reduce heat and stir in the lemon, fish stock, salt, pepper, cayenne, and hot red-pepper sauce. Simmer for 20 minutes.

Add the fish to the pan and continue to cook for 5 more minutes.

Blend saffron in 3 tablespoons of the soup. Remove the fillets from the soup and place on the toast in serving bowls. Spread the saffron mix on the fish and pour the soup over. Serve.

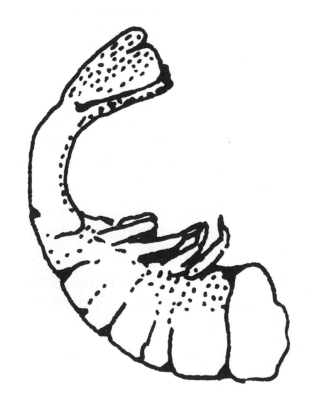

FRIED OKRA SOUP

serves 8

2 cups fresh lima beans
2 cups fresh corn
3 medium potatoes, peeled and diced
½ teaspoon black pepper
½ teaspoon salt
6 medium tomatoes, chopped
2 medium onions, chopped
2 celery stalks, chopped
1 tablespoon sugar
¼ head cabbage, chopped
½ pound bacon, diced
4 cups sliced fresh okra

•

In a large pot, combine the lima beans, corn, potatoes, pepper, salt, tomatoes, onions, celery and sugar. Cover the vegetables with water. Cover the pot and simmer for 45 minutes.

Stir in the cabbage and remove the pot from the heat.

Brown the bacon pieces in a large skillet, and add them to the pot. Reserve the drippings.

Fry the okra for 1 minute on each side in the bacon drippings. Gently stir the okra into the soup and serve.

GULF CRAB SOUP

serves 6

2 pounds crabmeat, finely chopped
5 cups fish stock
¼ cup lemon juice
1 cup unflavored breadcrumbs
1 onion, thinly sliced and separated into rings
3 sprigs parsley, coarsley chopped
1 bay leaf
½ teaspoon oregano
3 tablespoons softened butter
1 cup heavy cream
½ cup light cream
1 teaspoon salt
1 teaspoon cayenne pepper
2 tablespoons cooked shrimp, finely chopped
2 tablespoons sweet butter

•

In a large saucepan, combine the crabmeat, fish stock, lemon juice, breadcrumbs, onion, parsley, bay leaf and oregano. Bring the mixture to a boil, lower the heat and simmer for 20 minutes.

Strain the soup through a large sieve into another large saucepan. Mash the remaining crabmeat with a wooden spoon through the sieve and discard the remaining solids.

Add the softened butter and heat just to the boiling point.

Add the heavy cream, stirring constantly, and then add the light cream, salt and cayenne pepper. Heat soup through, but do not let it come to a boil. Just before serving, stir in the shrimp and sweet butter.

LOBSTER BOUILLABAISSE

serves 6

¼ cup olive oil
2 celery stalks, chopped
1 chopped onion
1 clove minced garlic
½ teaspoon thyme
1 bay leaf
3 chopped tomatoes
1 cup clam juice
1 cup dry white wine
¼ cup chopped parsley
½ teaspoon salt
½ teaspoon black pepper
1½ pounds firm white fish fillets, cut
into small pieces
3 lobster tails, sliced in half, shelled
and deveined

•

Heat the olive oil in a large saucepan, and sauté the celery, onion and garlic until soft but not brown.

Add the thyme, bay leaf, tomatoes, clam juice, wine and parsley and simmer for 15 minutes.

Add the fish fillet pieces and simmer for 5 minutes.

Add the lobster and simmer for 5 more minutes.

Add the salt and pepper, stir well and simmer an additional 5 minutes.

HAM HOCK AND CABBAGE SOUP

serves 6

1 to 1½ pounds smoked ham hocks
1 bay leaf
½ teaspoon black pepper
1½ cups whole stewed tomatoes
½ cabbage head, chopped
1 tablespoon vegetable oil
¼ pound beef, cubed
1 tablespoon flour
½ teaspoon salt
⅛ teaspoon Tabasco sauce

•

Put the ham hocks in a large pot and add the bay leaf and pepper. Add enough cold water to cover the ingredients. Bring the liquid to a boil, then reduce the heat, cover the pot and simmer for 1 hour.

Add the tomatoes and cabbage to the soup, stir well, and simmer for 1 hour longer.

Remove the ham hocks, cut the meat from the bones and chop it. Discard the bones; return the meat to the soup.

Heat the vegetable oil in a skillet. Add the cubed beef and sauté until lightly browned. Sprinkle the flour over the beef, stirring constantly with a wooden spoon. Spoon off 1 or 2 tablespoons of the soup broth and add to the skillet to loosen the gravy. Stir well. Add the beef and gravy to the soup. Stir in the salt and Tabasco sauce, cook for another 3 minutes, and serve.

MULLIGATAWNY

serves 6

1 3-pound chicken, cut into serving
pieces
4 tablespoons butter
½ cup chopped carrots
½ cup chopped green bell pepper
2 green apples, cored, peeled and
chopped
1 tablespoon flour
2 teaspoons curry powder
8 cups chicken broth
2 whole cloves
¼ cup fresh chopped parsley
1 tablespoon sugar
¼ teaspoon black pepper
1½ teaspoons salt

•

Melt the butter in a large saucepan and add the chicken. Sauté the chicken pieces for 8 minutes or until well browned.

Add the carrots, bell pepper and apples and stir well. Continue to sauté for 8 more minutes, stirring constantly. Add the flour and curry powder and blend well. Add the chicken broth, 1 cup at a time, stirring constantly. Add the cloves, parsley, sugar, pepper and salt, blend well and continue to cook over medium heat until the mixture begins to boil. Lower the heat, cover the saucepan and continue to cook for 30 minutes.

Remove the chicken from the soup and cool. Strain the soup through a large sieve, into another large sauce-pan and mash the vegetables through the sieve with a wooden spoon.

Heat the soup over low heat. While the soup is heating, skin and bone the chicken and cut into chunks. Add the chicken to the soup. Continue to heat until the soup simmers, then serve.

OYSTER CHOWDER

serves 4

½ pound bacon, diced
1 small onion, chopped
1½ cups boiling water
1 cup diced peeled potatoes
1 cup hot milk
1 dozen oysters, shelled
¼ cup oyster liquid
½ teaspoon salt
¼ teaspoon cayenne pepper

•

Slowly fry the bacon in a large deep skillet. Stir in the onion and continue to cook until the onion is soft and golden in color.

Add the boiling water and potatoes and simmer for 8 minutes. Add the milk, oysters, oyster liquid, salt and pepper and simmer for 10 minutes or until the oysters crinkle.

PUMPKIN SOUP

serves 6

1 small pumpkin
7 tablespoons butter
1 tablespoon sugar
1 teaspoon salt
½ teaspoon white pepper
6 cups hot milk

•

Cut the pumpkin into wedges and remove the seeds and skin from the meat. Put the pumpkin into a large pot and add enough water to cover. Bring to a boil and lower the heat. Simmer until the pumpkin is tender.

Drain the pumpkin, then using a wooden spoon, force it through a sieve back into the pot. Add the butter, sugar, salt, and pepper and simmer over low heat.

Gradually add the milk, stirring constantly until well blended. Simmer for 5 more minutes and serve.

SHRIMP AND RICE SOUP

serves 4

3 tablespoons olive oil
1 cup raw rice
2 tomatoes, chopped
1 cup cooked shrimp, shelled and deveined
3 cups hot water
1 teaspoon salt
1 teaspoon hot red-pepper sauce
lemon wedges

•

Heat the olive oil in a large heavy skillet until it is very hot. Add the raw rice and cook until the rice has turned golden brown, stirring constantly.

Add the tomatoes, shrimp, water, salt and hot red-pepper sauce, cover and simmer over low heat for 17 minutes, or until the rice is soft. Serve with lemon wedges on the side.

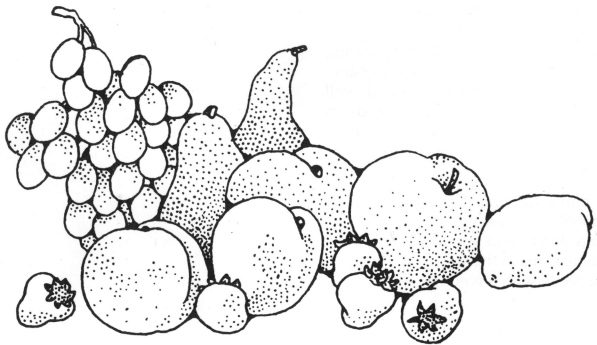

Corn and Shrimp Chowder

Seafood Salad

Deviled Eggs with Anchovies

Spiced Tomato Bouillon

serves 4

2½ cups stewed tomatoes
1 medium onion, thinly sliced and
separated into rings
1 teaspoon oregano
½ teaspoon celery seeds
½ teaspoon black pepper
½ teaspoon salt
¼ teaspoon crushed red pepper
2 cups bouillon
½ cup white wine

•

Combine the stewed tomatoes, onions, oregano, celery seeds, pepper, salt and crushed red pepper in a large skillet and blend well. Stir over medium heat until the mixture begins to bubble. Lower the heat and simmer for 15 minutes.

In a saucepan, combine the bouillon and white wine over low heat. When the tomato mix is ready, pour it through a large strainer into the bouillon. Heat the soup to a simmer and serve. *As supplied by Dorothy and Sharlyn Davis.*

She-Crab Soup

serves 6

6 tablespoons butter
1 tablespoon flour
2 cups milk
2 cups light cream
1½ pounds white crabmeat, flaked
1 tablespoon crab roe, if available
1 teaspoon grated lemon rind
¼ teaspoon mace
½ teaspoon salt
½ teaspoon black pepper
3 tablespoons dry sherry
1 tablespoon chopped parsley

•

In the top of a double boiler over briskly boiling water, melt the butter. When the butter has melted, sprinkle in the flour and blend well. Pour in the milk and cream, stirring constantly.

Add the grated lemon rind, mace, crabmeat and roe. Stir well and continue to cook for 20 minutes, stirring often.

Sprinkle in the salt and pepper and remove the double boiler from the stove. Allow the soup to stand over the hot water for 15 minutes.

Stir in the sherry and parsley and serve.

SPLIT PEA SOUP

serves 6

1½ cups dried green split peas
1 large hambone or hamhock
1 onion, stuck with 2 cloves
3 celery stalks, finely chopped
1 bay leaf
3 carrots, finely chopped
½ cup heavy cream

•

Cover the split peas with cold water to a depth of 1 inch and let stand overnight.

Drain the peas and place them in a large pot with the hambone, onion, celery, carrots and bay leaf. Add enough water to cover the vegetables and bone to a depth of 1 inch. Bring to a boil and reduce the heat. Simmer for 3 hours.

Remove the hambone, cutting any meat from it and returning it to the soup. Remove the cloves and bay leaf and pour the soup into a blender. Blend until smooth.

Pour the mixture back into the pot and bring to a simmer over low heat. Blend in the heavy cream, stirring constantly, and cook for 5 more minutes.

TOMATO SOUP WITH BEEF AND OKRA

serves 8

8 tablespoons butter
1 teaspoon oregano
1 garlic clove, finely chopped
2 pounds lean beef, cut into chunks
1½ pounds okra, thinly sliced
5 tomatoes, coarsely chopped
4 cups boiling water
2 cups cooked lima beans
2 cups cooked chicken meat, shredded
1 teaspoon salt
1 teaspoon black pepper

•

Melt the butter in a large deep pot. Sprinkle in the oregano and garlic. Blend well with the butter. Stir in the meat and brown on all sides.

Stir in the okra and tomatoes, and add enough water to cover the mixture entirely. Cover the pot and simmer for 1 hour.

Remove the cover and add the boiling water. Return to a boil and then lower the heat and simmer for 10 minutes. Add the lima beans, chicken, salt and pepper and blend well. Serve hot.

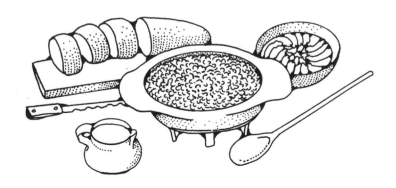

TOMATO BISQUE

serves 6

10 large ripe tomatoes
3 tablespoons butter
1 teaspoon oregano
2 medium onions, chopped
2 cups chicken broth
1 bay leaf
½ teaspoon sugar
½ teaspoon salt
½ teaspoon black pepper
1 cup light cream

•

Coarsely chop the tomatoes and set aside.

Melt the butter in a large, deep skillet and spinkle in the oregano. Stir in the onions and sauté until the onions are soft.

Add the chopped tomatoes and sauté until the tomatoes are soft. Remove from the heat and allow to cool slightly. Pour the mixture into a blender and blend until smooth. Pour the mixture back into the skillet and simmer over low heat.

Stir in the chicken broth, bay leaf, sugar, salt and pepper and mix well. Bring the mixture to a slow boil and whip in the light cream. Reduce the heat and simmer for 5 minutes before serving.

VEGETABLE BONE MARROW SOUP

serves a whole mess o' people

2 1-inch-thick slices beef shin bones, meat and marrow intact
3 meaty beef neckbones
1 tablespoon black pepper
5 quarts water or vegetable stock
2 large onions in chunks
5 tomatoes, coarsely chopped
½ cup dried green split peas
½ cup dried yellow split peas
½ cup small dried lima beans
½ cup small-grain barley
½ pound sliced okra
3 large carrots, sliced
3 celery stalks, sliced
1 cup fresh corn
1 cup uncooked string beans
2 small parsnips, peeled and sliced
2 tablespoons salt
2 tablespoons oregano

•

Place the shinbones, neckbones, and pepper in a 10-quart pot and add the water. Simmer briskly for one hour, skimming off any foam that forms.

Add the onions and the tomatoes and continue to cook for 30 minutes. Add the peas, lima beans and barley and continue to cook for 30 minutes. Remove any foam, cover and simmer for 1 hour.

Add the okra, carrots, celery, corn, beans, parsnips, salt and oregano and simmer for 1 more hour.

Remove the bones and any gristle before serving.

SALADS

APPLE-WALNUT SALAD

serves 10

12 apples, peeled, cored and diced
2 celery stalks, diced
1½ cups chopped walnuts
4 tablespoons seedless raisins
1½ cups mayonnaise
1 teaspoon lemon juice
½ teaspoon nutmeg

•

Combine the apples, celery, walnuts and raisins in a large bowl and set aside.

In a second bowl combine the mayonnaise, lemon juice and nutmeg. Fold the mayonnaise mixture into the apples and blend thoroughly. Chill for 20 minutes before serving.

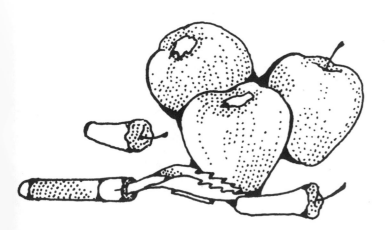

BEAN AND HERB SALAD

serves 6

4 cups water
1 cup dried navy or pea beans
1 teaspoon salt
1 tablespoon tarragon vinegar
2 teaspoons French-style mustard
½ teaspoon hot red-pepper sauce
½ teaspoon black pepper
⅓ cup olive oil
2 tablespoons chopped fresh basil
2 tablespoons finely chopped chives
2 mint leaves, finely chopped
2 garlic cloves, finely minced
1 large tomato, coarsely chopped

•

Combine the water and beans in a large saucepan and bring to a boil. Remove from the stove and allow the beans to soak in their water for 1 hour.

Add the salt to the saucepan and bring back to a boil. Reduce the heat and simmer for 1 hour. Remove the beans from the heat, drain and cool.

In a large salad bowl, combine the vinegar, mustard, hot red-pepper sauce and pepper. Add the olive oil in a steady stream and whisk until a smooth paste is formed.

In another mixing bowl, combine the basil, chives, mint and garlic. Mix well and add the tomatoes and beans. Toss gently but thoroughly. Pour the bean mixture into the bowl with the dressing and toss well. Serve.

COLD KIDNEY BEAN SALAD

serves 6

2 1-pound cans of kidney beans,
drained
7 scallions, finely chopped
½ cup finely chopped parsley
3 teaspoons finely chopped pimentos
3 garlic cloves, finely minced
6 tablespoons olive oil
3 tablespoons red wine vinegar
1 teaspoon lemon juice
1 teaspoon oregano
1 teaspoon salt
1 teaspoon black pepper

•

Drain the kidney beans well and pat dry. In a large salad bowl, combine the kidney beans, scallions, parsley, pimentos, and mix gently but thoroughly. Cover the bowl and refrigerate for 1 hour.

In a small bowl, combine the garlic, olive oil, vinegar, lemon juice, oregano, salt and pepper. Blend well, cover and let stand at room temperature.

At the end of the hour, pour the dressing over the salad and mix gently but thoroughly. Re-cover the salad and refrigerate for 3 hours. Remove from the refrigerator at least 30 minutes before serving.

CABBAGE SALAD

serves 6

½ head cabbage, shredded
½ head red cabbage, shredded
1 small green bell pepper, finely
chopped
1 small red bell pepper, finely chopped
¼ cup mayonnaise
¼ cup sour cream
3 tablespoons white wine vinegar
3 tablespoons sugar
½ teaspoon chili powder
½ teaspoon salt
½ teaspoon black pepper
¼ teaspoon cayenne pepper

•

Combine the cabbages and the bell peppers in a large bowl; cover and refrigerate for 2¼ hours.

In a mixing bowl, combine the mayonnaise, sour cream, vinegar, sugar, chili powder, salt, pepper and cayenne pepper and whisk until smooth. Refrigerate for 2 hours.

Pour the dressing over the salad and toss well before serving.

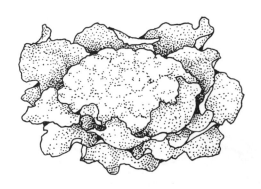

CHICKEN SALAD

serves 6

2 cups cooked chicken, diced and
chilled
2 tablespoons lemon juice
1 teaspoon oregano
½ teaspoon salt
½ teaspoon cayenne pepper
½ cup finely diced celery
½ cup diced apple
½ cup diced pickle
1 cup mayonnaise
½ teaspoon French-style mustard
1 teaspoon black pepper

•

Place the chicken in a bowl and
sprinkle with the lemon juice,
oregano, salt and cayenne pepper.
Cover and refrigerate for 1 hour.

Combine the celery, apple, pickles,
mayonnaise, mustard and pepper in
a second bowl and mix well. Refrigerate. Add the chicken to the bowl
and mix thoroughly before serving.

CRANBERRY ORANGE MOLD

serves 6

1 cup finely chopped fresh cranberries
1 cup sugar
½ cup boiling water
1 3-oz. package lemon-flavored gelatin
1 cup orange juice
2 teaspoons grated orange peel
1 cup drained crushed pineapple
1 cup chopped celery
½ cup chopped pecans

•

Mix the cranberries with the sugar
in a bowl and set aside for 2 hours.

Combine the water and gelatin in a
mixing bowl and stir until well
blended. Stir in orange juice, mix
well and refrigerate for 15 minutes or
until slightly thickened.

Stir the cranberries, orange peel,
pineapple, celery and pecans into
the gelatin mixture and mix well.
Pour into a mold and refrigerate
until set. Unmold onto a bed of
lettuce and serve.

CREAMY COLE SLAW

serves 8

1 cup sour cream
1 cup mayonnaise
3 tablespoons lemon juice
1 tablespoon celery seeds
1 tablespoon sugar
1 teaspoon salt
1 teaspoon cayenne pepper
¼ cup light cream
1 large head cabbage, shredded
½ small head red cabbage, shredded
3 carrots, coarsely grated

•

Combine the sour cream, mayonnaise, lemon juice, celery seeds, sugar, salt, cayenne pepper and light cream in a mixing bowl and whisk until smooth. Cover and refrigerate for 1 hour.

Combine the cabbages and carrots in a large bowl, cover and refrigerate for 1 hour. At the end of the hour, mix the dressing again, and then pour it over the cabbage.

Mix the salad well, cover and refrigerate for 2 hours before serving.

CUCUMBER SALAD

serves 6

2 cucumbers, very thinly sliced
1 small onion, very thinly sliced and broken into rings
½ cup sour cream
⅓ cup white wine vinegar
1 teaspoon salt
½ teaspoon black pepper
3 tablespoons sugar
½ teaspoon dry mustard
2 tablespoons light cream

•

Combine the cucumber slices and onion rings in a large bowl. Cover and refrigerate for 1 hour.

Combine the sour cream, vinegar, salt, pepper, mustard and light cream in a bowl and blend well. Cover and refrigerate.

Before serving, pour the dressing over the cucumbers and onions and toss well.

Fruit Salad for Y'All

serves everybody

3 cups water
1 cup sugar
½ cup honey
1 teaspoon grated orange peel
1 teaspoon grated lemon peel
6 peaches, peeled, seeded and cut into
wedges
1 cup mandarin orange segments
2 cups seedless grapes
4 green apples, cored and sliced into
wedges
1 honeydew melon, seeded and
scooped into balls
2 cups cherries, stemmed and pitted
1 cantaloupe, seeded and scooped into
balls
1 small watermelon, seeded and
scooped into balls
4 bananas
1 scoop cottage cheese per serving

•

Bring the water to a boil in a sauce-pan and add the sugar, honey, orange peel and lemon peel. Bring back to a boil, lower heat and simmer for 15 minutes.

In a giant bowl, combine the peaches, oranges, grapes, apples, honeydew, cherries, cantaloupe and water-melon. Mix gently but thoroughly.

Allow the sauce to cool slightly before pouring over the fruit and mixing well.

Slice the bananas in just before serving and toss gently again. Serve on beds of lettuce with a scoop of cottage cheese for each serving.

Garden Salad with Lemon Dressing

serves 6

½ head romaine lettuce
½ head soft lettuce
½ cup lemon juice
½ cup olive oil
1 teaspoon salt
1 teaspoon paprika
2 tablespoons honey
6 radishes, thinly sliced
1 large carrot, thinly sliced
3 scallions, chopped
¼ cup finely chopped parsley
1 tomato coarsely chopped

•

Rinse the lettuce leaves and drain well. Wrap the leaves in paper towels and refrigerate for 2 hours.

Combine the lemon juice, olive oil, salt, paprika and honey in a bowl and blend well. Cover and refrigerate.

Combine the radishes carrots, scallions, parsley and tomato in a large bowl and toss well. Cover and refrigerate.

Break the lettuce leaves into the large bowl with the vegetables and pour the dressing over the top. Toss gently but thoroughly and serve.

GAZPACHO SALAD

serves 4

1 large cucumber, thinly sliced
1 tomato, thinly sliced
1 onion, thinly sliced
2 tablespoons chopped pimento
3 tablespoons white wine vinegar
1 garlic clove, minced
2 tablespoons olive oil
1 hard-cooked egg
½ teaspoon salt
½ teaspoon black pepper
4 saltine crackers

•

Combine the cucumber, tomato, onion and pimento in a bowl, toss well, cover and refrigerate. Combine the vinegar and garlic in a small bowl and set aside. Combine the oil and the egg yolk in another small bowl and blend well.

Chop the egg white and add it to the yolk mixture with the salt and pepper. Combine the vinegar mixture and the oil mixture and pour them over the vegetables. Refrigerate for 1 hour. Crumble in the crackers just before serving.

GINGER ALE SALAD

serves 6

½ cup sliced peaches
½ cup grapefruit segments, quartered
½ cup cherries, stemmed and pitted
½ cup canned crushed pineapple, with juice
½ cup seedless grapes
½ cup water
½ cup slivered unsalted almonds
2 tablespoons lemon juice
2 tablespoons unflavored gelatin
½ teaspoon ground ginger
½ teaspoon salt
½ cup mayonnaise
2 cups ginger ale

•

Combine the peaches, grapefruit, cherries, pineapple, grapes and water in a large bowl. Stir well and pour off all the liquid into a skillet.

Add the almonds to the fruit, mix well, cover and refrigerate. Add the gelatin to the juice in the skillet and let stand for 2 minutes. Blend well and bring to a slow simmer.

Stir into the skillet the lemon juice, ginger, salt, mayonnaise and ginger ale. Mix well. Simmer for 3 minutes and remove from the heat.

Chill the sauce until it starts to become solid. Pour the sauce over the fruit and mix well. Pour the mixture into a mold and chill until set. Unmold onto a bed of lettuce.

HOT POTATO SALAD

serves 6

½ pound bacon, diced
6 potatoes, boiled, peeled and diced
½ cup diced cooked celery
1 onion, finely chopped
¼ cup vinegar
1 tablespoon sugar
½ teaspoon salt
½ teaspoon celery seeds
¼ teaspoon paprika
½ teaspoon black pepper
½ teaspoon dry mustard
1 tablespoon chopped parsley

•

Cook the bacon in a large skillet until well done. Remove the bacon with a slotted spoon and drain on paper towels.

Add the potatoes, celery and onion to the skillet and simmer over low heat for 5 minutes. Combine the vinegar, sugar, celery seeds, paprika, pepper, mustard and parsley in a bowl and blend well.

Pour the dressing over the potatoes in the skillet and simmer for 5 more minutes. Serve immediately.

GREEN BEAN SALAD

serves 6

2 pounds whole, fresh green beans
½ pound bacon, coarsely diced
1 small red onion, thinly sliced and
broken into rings
2 scallions, chopped
½ cup olive oil
6 tablespoons red wine vinegar
1 teaspoon oregano
½ teaspoon salt
½ teaspoon black pepper

•

Trim the green beans and cook them in a large pot of boiling salted water for 4 minutes. Drain the beans well and rinse with cold water. Wrap the beans in paper towels and refrigerate for 2 hours.

In a skillet, fry the bacon until well done, but not blackened. Drain the bacon and place it in a salad bowl. Add the red onion rings, scallions, olive oil, vinegar, oregano, salt and pepper and toss well. Cover the bowl and refrigerate.

Just before serving, add the beans to the salad bowl and toss gently but thoroughly.

MOLDED SHRIMP SALAD

serves 6

1 ⅔ cups boiling water
1 3-oz package lemon-flavored gelatin
1 cup cooked whole shrimp, shelled
and deveined
½ cup finely chopped celery
¼ cup chopped stuffed olives
¼ cup chopped sweet pickles
¼ teaspoon salt
lettuce leaves
7 tablespoons mayonnaise
1 tablespoon lemon juice

•

Add the boiling water to the gelatin in a large bowl and stir until the gelatin has dissolved. Cool.

Add the shrimp, celery, olives, pickles, and salt. Mix well and pour into a gelatin mold. Refrigerate until set.

Arrange the lettuce leaves on a platter. In a small bowl combine the mayonnaise and lemon juice and blend well.

Unmold the gelatin mixture onto the lettuce. Spoon the mayonnaise into the center of the mold before serving.

SEAFOOD SALAD

serves 4

1 cut whole cooked shrimp, shelled and
deveined
½ cup coarsely chopped cooked lobster
½ cup flaked cooked crabmeat
½ cup halved cooked scallops
1 cup mandarin orange segments
¼ cup black olives, pitted
¼ cup green olives, pitted
2 tablespoons white wine vinegar
1 tablespoon lemon juice
1 teaspoon French-style mustard
½ teaspoon salt
½ teaspoon black pepper
1 tablespoon chopped fresh parsley
½ cup olive oil

•

Combine the shrimp, crabmeat, lobster and scallops in a bowl. Cover and refrigerate. Line a large bowl with lettuce leaves and set aside.

In another bowl, combine the orange segments and olives and toss. In a small bowl combine the vinegar, lemon juice, mustard, salt, pepper and parsley, and whisk in the olive oil. Pour the dressing over the orange mix and toss well.

Pour the seafood into the salad mix and toss gently before turning into the bowl lined with lettuce. Serve.

PAPAYA SEAFOOD SALAD

serves 4

2 large ripe papayas, chilled
1 cup chopped cooked shrimp
1 cup flaked cooked crabmeat
1 cup finely chopped celery
2 scallions, chopped
½ teaspoon curry powder
½ cup mayonnaise
3 tablespoons lime juice
1 lime, quartered

•

Slice the papayas in half lengthwise and scoop out the seeds. Place each in a serving dish and set aside.

Combine the shrimp, crabmeat, celery and scallions in a bowl and toss together. Combine the curry powder, mayonnaise and lime juice in a small bowl and whisk until smooth.

Pour the dressing over the seafood mix and toss gently but thoroughly. Spoon equal portions of the salad into each papaya half and serve with a lime wedge.

RED PEPPER AND CELERY ROOT SALAD

serves 12

6 red bell peppers, julienned
3 large celery roots, julienned
6 tablespoons red wine vinegar
3 tablespoons lemon juice
3 tablespoons French-style mustard
3 teaspoons dried chervil
1½ teaspoons dried tarragon
3 teaspoons finely chopped parsley
¾ cup olive oil
1 teaspoon black pepper

•

Combine the peppers and the celery roots in a large bowl and set aside.

Combine the vinegar, lemon juice, mustard, chervil, tarragon and parsley in a small bowl and blend well. Whisk in the olive oil and pepper until smooth.

Pour the dressing over the vegetables and mix well. Cover and refrigerate for at least 4 hours before serving.

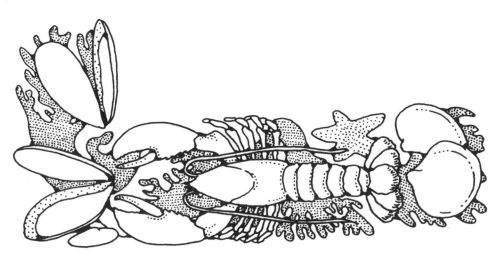

SHRIMP AND AVOCADO COCKTAIL

serves 4

1½ pounds whole cooked shrimp,
shelled and deveined
1 cup ketchup
1 tablespoon lemon juice
1 tablespoon chili sauce
1 tablespoon prepared horseradish
1 tablespoon sugar
1 teaspoon onion juice
¼ teaspoon salt
½ teaspoon Worcestershire sauce
¼ teaspoon hot red-pepper sauce
2 large avocados
lettuce leaves
lemon wedges

•

Place the shrimp in a large bowl and cover with crushed ice. Refrigerate for 1 hour.

Combine the ketchup, lemon juice, chili sauce, horseradish, onion juice, salt, Worcestershire sauce and hot red-pepper sauce in a bowl and whisk until well blended. Refrigerate sauce.

Place the avocados on a cutting board and slice in half lengthwise. Remove seeds and place meat-side down on the cutting board. Pinch off the skins. Slice the avocados and arrange them on beds of lettuce on four serving plates. Remove the shrimp from the ice and toss them with the sauce. Spoon equal portions over the avocado slices and serve with lemon wedges.

SHRIMP AND BEAN SALAD

serves 4

1 1-pound can white beans
1 1-pound can kidney beans
1 pound whole cooked shrimp, shelled and deveined
1 small green bell pepper, finely chopped
1 small red bell pepper, finely chopped
2 scallions, chopped
2 tablespoons finely chopped pimento
½ teaspoon salt
½ teaspoon black pepper
¼ teaspoon cayenne pepper
¼ cup white wine vinegar
½ cup olive oil

•

Place the beans in a colander and rinse well under cold running water. Drain well.

Combine the beans, shrimp, green bell pepper, red bell pepper, scallions and pimentos in a large bowl and toss gently. Sprinkle with salt, pepper and cayenne pepper and toss again.

In a separate bowl, whisk together the olive oil and vinegar. Pour the dressing over the salad and toss well. Refrigerate, covered, and toss again before serving.

SPICY GARBANZO BEAN SALAD

serves 4

1 1-pound can garbanzo beans
(chickpeas), drained
1 small white onion, finely chopped
1 tablespoon finely chopped parsley
2 carrots, cooked and diced
¼ cup olive oil
2 tablespoons cider vinegar
1 teaspoon salt
1 teaspoon black pepper
1½ teaspoons dried hot red-pepper
flakes
¼ teaspoon cayenne pepper
1 tablespoon lemon juice
lettuce leaves

•

Drain the garbanzos well and rinse under cold water. Place the beans in a covered bowl and refrigerate for 1 hour.

Combine the onion, parsley, carrots, olive oil, vinegar, salt, pepper, red pepper, cayenne pepper and lemon juice in a large salad bowl and toss well. Cover the bowl and refrigerate.

Add the beans to the salad bowl and toss well. Cover and refrigerate for 1 hour before serving.

SPICY VEGETABLE SALAD

serves 4

1 large cucumber, peeled and sliced
½ cup cooked lima beans
½ cup cooked, diced carrots
8 pimento-stuffed green olives, sliced
¾ cup mayonnaise
1 tablespoon chili sauce
½ teaspoon sugar
1 teaspoon prepared horseradish
½ teaspoon salt
½ teaspoon black pepper
1 small head lettuce, torn into small
pieces
2 tablespoons olive oil
1 tomato, finely chopped
4 scallions, chopped

•

In a large salad bowl combine the cucumber, lima beans, carrots, olives, mayonnaise, chili sauce, sugar, horseradish, salt and pepper. Mix well.

In another bowl, combine the lettuce and olive oil. Toss well and add the scallions and tomato. Toss again. Add the lettuce mixture to the salad bowl and toss again before serving.

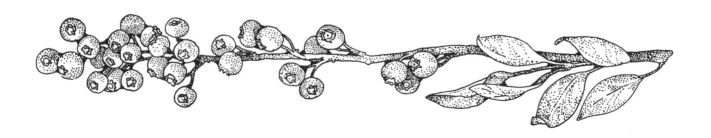

SOUTHERN-STYLE POTATO SALAD

serves 6

6 medium potatoes
½ cup finely chopped sweet pickles
1 medium onion, finely chopped
½ cup cider vinegar
½ cup finely chopped celery
1 teaspoon French-style mustard
1 teaspoon salt
½ teaspoon black pepper
1½ cups mayonnaise
¼ cup finely chopped fresh parsley
2 tablespoons olive oil

•

Place the potatoes in a large pot and cover with boiling salted water. Over a low heat simmer, uncovered for 40 minutes. While the potatoes cook, combine the pickles, onion, vinegar, celery, mustard, salt, pepper and mayonnaise in a large bowl and toss well. Cover and refrigerate.

When the potatoes are soft, pour them into a colander and rinse under cold running water. When the potatoes are cool enough to handle, cut them in half lengthwise and lay them, meat-side down, on a cutting board. Remove the skins and dice.

Place the potatoes in a bowl and gently toss with the olive oil and parsley. Cover and refrigerate.

About 20 minutes before serving, toss the two mixtures together.

THREE-BEAN SALAD

serves 6

1 1-pound can garbanzos, drained
1 1-pound can kidney beans, drained
1 1-pound can green beans, drained
½ cup olive oil
¼ cup chopped fresh parsley
1 small red onion, sliced thin and separated into rings
3 scallions, chopped
2 tablespoons chopped pimentos
2 garlic cloves, finely chopped
2 tablespoons lemon juice
4 tablespoons red wine vinegar
1 teaspoon oregano
1 teaspoon salt
1 teaspoon black pepper

•

Drain the beans well and rinse with cold water. Drain again and place in a large bowl. Pour the olive oil over the beans and gently toss. Add the parsley and gently toss again. Cover the bowl and refrigerate for 1 hour.

In a separate bowl combine the red onion, scallions, pimentos, garlic, lemon juice, vinegar, oregano, salt and pepper. Toss well, cover the dish and refrigerate.

After the beans have been in the refrigerator for 1 hour, pour the onion mix over the beans and toss gently but thoroughly. Cover the dish and refrigerate for 2 hours before serving.

Cucumber Salad

Shrimp and Corn Souffle

Corned Beef Hash

WILTED LETTUCE

serves 4

6 slices bacon, diced
⅓ cup cider vinegar
2 heads lettuce, torn into
medium-small pieces
¼ cup chopped scallions
¼ teaspoon salt
¼ teaspoon black pepper
2 hard-cooked eggs, chopped

•

Sauté the bacon pieces in a large skillet. When the bacon is crisp, add the vinegar to the skillet. Cook over very low heat until heated through.

Remove the skillet from the heat and add the lettuce, scallions, salt and pepper. Toss for 1 to 2 minutes, or until the lettuce is wilted. Add the chopped eggs and toss again. Place in a bowl and serve immediately.

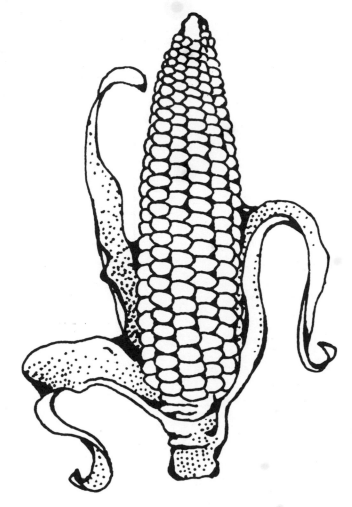

VEGETABLES

BAKED BEANS

serves 6

1 pound navy beans
1 medium onion, diced
2½ cups stewed tomatoes
1½ cups brown sugar, loosely packed
¼ pound bacon, cut into thirds

•

Soak the beans in 8 cups cold water for 8 hours or overnight. Drain the beans, put them in a saucepan and add the onion. Cover with water and parboil for 1 hour. Drain the liquid and reserve. Preheat the oven to 325°F. Add the tomatoes and brown sugar to the beans, mix well and place in a covered, ungreased casserole dish. Lay the bacon strips over the bean mixture. Cover and bake for 4 hours, turning the bacon every hour.

As the moisture evaporates, add the reserved liquid to the dish to keep the beans from drying out. Do not stir. Uncover the dish and raise the oven temperature to 375°F. Cook for 1 more hour, turning the bacon after 30 minutes to brown both sides. Stir well and serve.

BLACKEYED PEAS

serves 8

2 pounds fresh blackeyed peas
¼ pound bacon, diced
½ teaspoon salt
½ teaspoon black pepper
½ teaspoon cayenne pepper
2 tablespoons chopped fresh parsley

•

Place the peas in a saucepan and cover with salted water. Bring to a boil and lower the heat. Simmer until tender, about 15 minutes.

While the peas simmer, fry the bacon in a skillet. Remove the bacon with a slotted spoon and drain on paper towels. Discard all but 5 table-spoons of the bacon drippings. Blend the salt, pepper and cayenne pepper. Drain the peas and add them to the skillet. Stir in the parsley and simmer over low heat for 3 minutes. Add the bacon, toss and serve.

NEW YEAR'S BLACKEYED PEAS IN DRESSING

serves 8

1 pound dried blackeyed peas or cowpeas
4 ounces diced salt pork
2 red onions, diced
3 garlic cloves, crushed
2 teaspoons hot red pepper flakes
1 cup peanut oil
1 cup cider vinegar
1 tablespoon Worcestershire sauce
¼ cup brown sugar
1 teaspoon dried basil
pimento-stuffed green olives

•

Rinse the blackeyed peas well. Put the peas in a large bowl with 6 cups of cold water and soak for 8 hours or overnight. Drain well.

Put the peas into a large pot and add the salt pork. Add 3 quarts of cold water, cover the pot and cook over moderate heat for 1¼ hours, or until the peas are tender. Drain well.

In a large deep bowl, toss the peas, onions, garlic and red pepper flakes together.

Mix the oil, vinegar, Worcestershire sauce, brown sugar and basil in a bowl. Blend well.

Pour the dressing over the peas, cover the bowl and marinate in the refrigerator for a day before serving.

Serve cold, topped with slices of Spanish olives.

BOILED PINTO BEANS

serves 8

2 cups dried pinto beans
12 cups water
1 medium-sized onion
2 garlic cloves, crushed
1 teaspoon salt
¼ teaspoon sugar

•

Rinse the dried beans well under cold running water. Place them in a large bowl with 6 cups cold water and soak overnight.

Drain the soaked beans and place them in a large saucepan. Add 6 cups water, the onion and garlic. Bring the water to a boil over high heat. Reduce the heat and simmer 3½ to 4 hours, partially covered.

Add the salt and sugar. Continue to simmer 30 minutes longer or until the beans are tender but still intact. Drain the beans and serve hot.

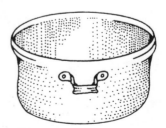

Cowboy Beans

serves 6

2 cups dried pinto beans
1 ham bone
1 hot red pepper pod
1 teaspoon salt
¼ pound salt pork, chopped
1 large onion, chopped
1 garlic clove, chopped
4 tomatoes, chopped
½ teaspoon ground cumin
1½ teaspoons chili powder
1 teaspoon salt

•

Rinse the dried beans well under cold running water. Place beans in a large pot with 6 cups cold water. Soak overnight.

In the morning add the ham bone, red chili pepper, and salt to the undrained beans. Bring the mixture to a boil. Reduce the heat and cover. Simmer gently until the beans are tender about 3 to 4 hours. Drain and reserve 1 cup of the liquid.

When the beans are almost done, heat the salt pork in a large skillet. Stir in the onion and garlic and cook for 5 minutes. Add the tomatoes, reserved bean liquid, cumin, chili powder and salt. Mix well. Cook over low heat, stirring frequently, for 45 minutes.

Mix in the beans and continue to simmer for 20 minutes longer. Remove from heat and serve.

Green Beans and Bacon

serves 6

2 tablespoons butter
6 slices bacon, cut into ½-inch pieces
1½ pounds fresh green beans, trimmed and cut into 1-inch pieces
½ teaspoon black pepper

•

Melt the butter in a large skillet over moderate heat. Add the bacon and sauté it until crisp, about 10 minutes. Set the skillet aside.

Bring a large pan of water to a boil over high heat. Add the beans and cook them until tender-crisp, 7 to 10 minutes.

Drain the beans well. Add them to the skillet and toss them quickly with the bacon and butter over high heat until they are coated with the butter and bacon fat and well mixed. Season with pepper before serving.

RED BEANS AND RICE

serves 8 to 10

1 pound dried red kidney beans
2 small ham hocks
2 tablespoons vegetable oil
1 tablespoon finely chopped garlic
2 cups finely chopped onions
1 cup finely chopped green peppers
1 cup finely chopped celery
¼ cup finely chopped parsley
¼ teaspoon cayenne pepper
1 bay leaf
½ teaspoon dried thyme
1 teaspoon Tabasco sauce
1 teaspoon sugar
salt to taste
black pepper to taste
1 cup chopped canned tomatoes
1 pound smoked sausage, cut into thick slices
1 cup finely chopped scallions

•

Put the beans and ham hocks in a large bowl. Add 8 cups cold water and soak the beans and ham hocks overnight.

Drain the beans and ham hocks and put them into a large heavy pot or Dutch oven. Add 8 cups cold water and bring the liquid to a boil over moderate heat.

Heat the oil in a skillet and add the garlic, onions, green peppers and celery. Sauté, stirring often, for 3 minutes. Add the mixture to the beans. Add the parsley, cayenne pepper, bay leaf, thyme, Tabasco sauce, sugar, salt, black pepper and tomatoes to the beans. Stir well. Cook the beans, uncovered, over moderate heat for 2 hours. Stir

occasionally. After the beans have cooked for 1½ hours, add the sausage slices.

Just before the beans are ready to serve, remove 1 cup of beans, with cooking liquid, from the pot. Purée the removed beans in a blender or food processor and return the purée to the pot. Stir well.

Serve the beans over rice in deep soup bowls. Garnish each serving with chopped scallions.

GLAZED CARROTS

serves 6

2 pounds baby carrots, washed, rinsed and drained
6 tablespoons butter
4 tablespoons sugar
2 tablespoons honey
½ teaspoon cinnamon
1 tablespoon fresh chopped parsley

•

Place the carrots in a saucepan and cover with salted water. Bring to a boil and simmer for 15 minutes.

Melt the butter in a skillet and blend in the sugar, honey and cinnamon. Drain the carrots and add them to the skillet. Stir well but gently to coat thoroughly. Sauté, stirring gently, for 5 minutes over low heat.

Sprinkle with parsley, toss and serve.

Down-Home Carrot Casserole

serves 6

⅔ cup raw long-grain rice
2 cups milk
1 cup water
4 eggs
3 tablespoons sugar
1¼ teaspoons salt
¼ cup chopped pecans
3 cups coarsely shredded carrots
butter

•

In the top of a double boiler, combine the rice, milk and water. Cook, covered, over boiling water for 35 minutes or until the rice is tender. Drain any liquid that is left.

Preheat the oven to 350°F.

In a mixing bowl beat the eggs. Add the sugar and salt. Continue beating until the mixture is light and fluffy. Stir in the cooked rice, chopped pecans and shredded carrots. Mix well.

Butter a 1½-quart baking dish. Put the carrot mixture in the dish and dot with butter. Bake for 1 hour. Serve hot.

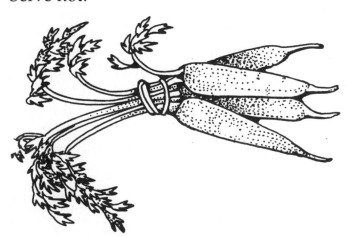

Cauliflower au Gratin

serves 6

1 large cauliflower
2 tablespoons butter
⅓ cup sifted flour
2 cups milk, scalded
½ teaspoon salt
½ teaspoon black pepper
¼ teaspoon nutmeg
1 cup grated cheddar cheese
¼ cup unflavored breadcrumbs
2 tablespoons chopped parsley
2 butter pats, broken into pieces

•

Trim and wash the cauliflower. Separate the flowerets and cook in a large pot of boiling salted water for 15 minutes, or until tender but not soft. Drain well. Arrange the flowerets in a shallow ovenproof dish. Preheat the broiler.

Melt the butter in a skillet over low heat. Stir in the flour until well blended. Stir in the milk. Add the salt, pepper, nutmeg and cheese, stirring constantly. Pour the cheese sauce over the cauliflower and sprinkle with the breadcrumbs and parsley. Dot with the remaining butter and place under the broiler. Broil slowly and remove when the sauce begins to brown.

CORN AND GREEN CHILI SOUFFLÉ

serves 6

5 eggs, separated
3 canned whole green chili peppers,
peeled and seeded
1 cup corn kernels
½ teaspoon salt
½ teaspoon black pepper
½ teaspoon chili powder

•

Preheat the oven to 400°F. Butter a 1½-quart soufflé or casserole dish

Place the egg yolks, whole chilis, corn, salt, pepper and chili powder in a blender. Process on medium speed for 1 minute.

In a separate bowl, beat the egg whites until stiff but not dry. Fold the corn mixture into the egg whites and blend thoroughly.

Turn the mixture into the soufflé dish and bake for 30 minutes. Serve immediately.

SOUTHERN STRING BEANS

serves 6

4 slices diced bacon
2 cups water
1 small onion, sliced into rings
½ teaspoon salt
2 pounds green beans, trimmed
2 tablespoons chopped pimento

•

Place the bacon in a saucepan and add the water. Bring to a boil and cook for 10 minutes. Add the onions and salt and cook for 1½ minutes. Add the beans and cook at a boil for 7 minutes. Drain off the liquid and stir in the pimentos before serving.

SOUTH CAROLINA CORN PIE

serves 6

4 cups fresh corn
⅓ cup butter, melted
3 eggs
1½ cups milk
½ cup evaporated milk
2 teaspoons sugar
½ teaspoon salt

•

Preheat the oven to 325°F. Place corn in a medium-sized casserole dish. Stir in the melted butter. In a separate bowl, beat the eggs until frothy. Add the milk, sugar and salt to the eggs and pour over the corn. Pour the evaporated milk over the mixture and stir briefly.

Bake for 40 minutes. Let cool slightly before serving.

Fried Corn

serves 4

6 ears corn
¼ pound bacon, finely diced
2 tablespoons flour, sifted
1 tablespoon sugar
1 cup water
½ teaspoon salt
½ teaspoon black pepper

•

Shuck the corn and remove any silk. With a small paring knife cut through the center of each row of kernels. Scrape the cut kernels off the ears into a bowl. Scrape the juice from the cob.

Fry the bacon in a deep skillet over medium heat. When the bacon is almost well done, add the corn, stirring well. Stir in the flour, water and sugar and continue to stir while heating through. Add the salt and pepper and raise the heat to medium high.

Stir constantly until corn begins to brown. Remove from stove and serve.

Baked Eggplant Casserole

serves 8

2 large eggplants
⅓ cup flour, sifted
⅓ cup cracker meal
⅓ cup grated Parmesan cheese
½ teaspoon paprika
½ teaspoon garlic powder
½ teaspoon salt
½ teaspoon black pepper
2 eggs
1 cup tomato consommé
1 cup evaporated milk
1 cup olive oil
1 cup shredded cheddar cheese
1 cup shredded Monterey Jack cheese

•

Trim the eggplants and cut into half-inch slices. Combine the flour, cracker meal, Parmesan cheese, paprika, garlic powder, salt and pepper in a bowl and blend well. Beat the eggs in another bowl. Combine the tomato consommé and evaporated milk in a saucepan and place over very low heat.

Preheat the oven to 325°F. Heat the olive oil in a deep skillet over medium heat.

Dip the eggplant slices into the egg and coat well in the flour mixture. Cook in the oil on both sides for 1 minute each. Drain on paper towels and place in a large, buttered casserole dish in layers until all of the eggplant slices are used. Pour the tomato sauce over the eggplant slices and top with the cheddar and Monterey Jack cheeses. Bake, uncovered, for 30 minutes. Let cool slightly before serving.

CORN OYSTERS

serves 6

3 cups corn kernels
3 eggs, well beaten
1½ teaspoons baking powder
½ teaspoon salt
¼ teaspoon black pepper
3 tablespoons light cream
⅓ cup flour
butter

•

In a large bowl combine the corn, eggs, baking powder, salt, pepper, cream and flour. Beat the mixture until well blended.

Melt 1 tablespoon butter on a griddle. Drop the corn mixture by rounded tablespoons onto the griddle. Fry until the oysters are golden brown on both sides, about 3 to 4 minutes a side. Fry only as many corn oysters as will fit easily on the griddle at one time. Add more butter as needed. Serve hot.

COLLARD GREENS

serves 12

1½ quarts water
1 teaspoon hot red pepper flakes
2 ham hocks
8 pounds collard greens, trimmed
2 teaspoons sugar
½ cup cider vinegar
1 teaspoon salt
1 teaspoon black pepper

•

Combine the water, red pepper and ham hocks in a large pot and boil for 1 hour. Trim off any yellow or damaged leaves and tough stems from the greens and wash several times until rinse water is clear.

Cut the leaves into smaller pieces. After 1 hour of cooking, add the leaves, sugar, vinegar, salt and pepper to the pot. Cover the pot and cook rapidly for 30 minutes. Drain off any excess liquid. You might want to stir in some chopped raw onions before serving.

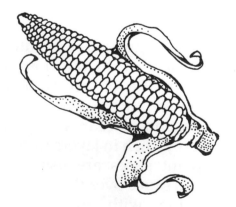

Stuffed Eggplant

serves 8

**2 large eggplants, halved lengthwise
3 tablespoons butter
2 onions, diced
3 green bell peppers, diced
8 ripe tomatoes, peeled and diced
½ teaspoon salt
½ teaspoon black pepper
5 ounces cheddar cheese, shredded
5 ounces Monterey Jack cheese, shredded
¾ cup unflavored breadcrumbs**

•

Preheat the oven to 425°F. Carefully scoop out the eggplant from the skin, leaving a thin shell one-quarter inch thick. Place the eggplant meat in a saucepan with salted boiling water to cover and cook until tender.

While the eggplant is cooking, melt the butter in a skillet and sauté the onions and peppers. As the onions become translucent, add the tomatoes, salt and pepper. Simmer for 10 minutes.

When the eggplant meat is tender, drain and return to the saucepan. Add half the cheddar and Monterey Jack cheeses. Stir constantly as the cheese begins to melt. Add the breadcrumbs and continue to stir. As the breadcrumbs become covered with the cheese, add the vegetable mixture to the saucepan, using a slotted spoon. Stir well and add just enough of the liquid from the skillet to make a moist, but not watery, mixture. Fill the eggplant shells with the mixture and bake in a lightly greased baking dish for 45 minutes. Top the eggplants with equal amounts of the reserved cheese and bake for 15 minutes more.

Mixed Greens

serves 12

**2 large ham hocks
8 cups water
5 pounds mustard greens, trimmed
3 pounds turnip greens, trimmed
2 pounds small white turnips, peeled and quartered
1 teaspoon salt
1 teaspoon black pepper**

•

Boil the ham hocks in the water in a large pot for 1 hour. While the ham hocks cook, trim off any yellow or damaged leaves from the greens. Remove stems and wash leaves three or four times until the rinse water is clear.

After the ham hocks have cooked for 1 hour, add the greens and turnips to the pot and bring back to a boil. Cook for 25 minutes and then use a large fork and knife to cut the leaves while they are still in the pot. Add the salt and pepper and simmer for 15 minutes.

MUSTARD GREENS WITH NEW POTATOES

serves 6

2 pounds fresh mustard greens
2 ounces thinly sliced salt pork
12 small new potatoes, quartered
1½ teaspoons salt
½ teaspoon sugar
¼ teaspoon black pepper

•

Wash the mustard greens thoroughly. Cut off and discard any tough stems and discolored leaves. Cut the greens into pieces 2 to 3 inches long.

Place the salt pork in a large skillet filled with water to a depth of 1 inch. Cover and simmer for 40 to 50 minutes or until the pork is tender.

Add the potatoes to the pork and cook for 5 to 7 minutes. Add more water if necessary. Add the mustard greens, salt and sugar. Cover and cook over medium heat for 15 minutes or until the mustard greens are tender. Do no overcook. Season with pepper and toss well. Serve hot.

TURNIP GREENS AND HAM HOCK

serves 6 to 8

1 1¾-pound ham hock
2 quarts water
2 bunches turnip greens with turnips
1 teaspoon salt
1 tablespoon sugar
black pepper to taste

•

Wash the ham hock and place it in a large heavy pot. Add the water and bring to a boil. Lower the heat and simmer gently for 35 to 45 minutes or until the ham hock is tender.

Wash and trim the turnip greens. Discard any discolored leaves. Peel the turnips and cut them in half.

Add the turnip greens, turnips, salt and sugar to the pot with the ham hock. Bring to a boil. Lower the heat and simmer 35 to 45 minutes or until the greens and turnips are tender.

Remove from the heat. Season to taste with black pepper. Spoon the greens and turnips into a serving bowl and serve hot.

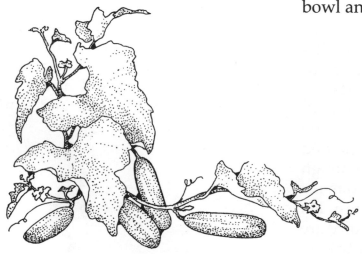

Fried Grits

serves 4

5 cups water
1 teaspoon salt
1 cup regular white hominy grits
1 tablespoon butter
2 eggs, beaten
1 cup fine unflavored breadcrumbs
4 tablespoons butter

•

Bring the water and salt to a boil and stir in the grits. Stir constantly until the water boils again. Reduce the heat, cover the pot and simmer for 25 minutes. Stir in the butter and allow the mixture to cool slightly. Pour the mixture into a loaf pan and chill overnight.

Slice the grits loaf into 12 slices. Dip the slices into the egg and then coat with the breadcrumbs. Melt the butter in a skillet and fry the grits slices for 3 minutes on each side. Serve with maple syrup.

Hominy

serves 4

2 cups whole hominy
3 cups water
2 teaspoons salt
½ cup light cream
½ cup butter

•

Place the whole hominy in a large bowl, cover with the water and soak overnight, covered. Drain the hominy and place in a large pot. Add the water and salt and simmer for 6 hours, or until the hominy is tender. Add the cream and butter, stir well and simmer for 1½ to 2 hours.

Hominy Grits

serves 4

5 cups water
1 teaspoon salt
1 cup regular white hominy grits
1 tablespoon butter
½ teaspoon salt
½ teaspoon black pepper

•

Put the water in a large pot and bring to a boil. Add the salt and hominy grits, stir and bring back to a boil. Stir constantly. When the water begins to boil again, lower the heat, cover and simmer for 25 minutes. Stir in the butter, salt and pepper and blend well.

Note: Sugar may be substituted for the salt and pepper.

CORN AND OKRA MIX

serves 4

4 strips bacon
1 onion, finely chopped
1 cup fresh okra, thinly sliced
3 cups fresh corn
3 tomatoes, peeled and diced
1 teaspoon sugar
½ teaspoon black pepper
1 teaspoon salt
½ teaspoon hot red-pepper sauce

•

Fry the bacon in a large skillet until it is crisp.

Drain on paper towels and reserve. Reserve 4 tablespoons of the bacon drippings and discard the rest.

Add the okra, corn and onion to the hot bacon drippings and sauté for 10 minutes. Add the tomatoes, sugar, pepper, salt and hot red-pepper sauce, stir well, and simmer for 5 minutes. Stir well, cover the skillet and simmer over low heat for 20 minutes. Sprinkle with crumbled bacon and serve.

GRITS AND CHEESE CASSEROLE

serves 6

5 cups water
1 teaspoon salt
1 cup regular white hominy grits
½ cup butter, cut into pieces
2 cups grated cheddar cheese
3 eggs, beaten
½ teaspoon hot red-pepper sauce
½ teaspoon salt
½ teaspoon black pepper

•

Bring the water and salt to a boil and stir in the grits. Stir constantly and bring to a boil again. Lower the heat and simmer, covered, for 25 minutes. Stir in the butter and cheese and allow to cool. Preheat the oven to 350°F.

When cool, stir in the eggs, red-pepper sauce, salt and pepper. Turn the mixture into a buttered casserole dish. Bake, covered, for 35 minutes.

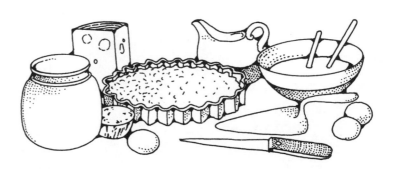

FRIED OKRA

serves 6

2 pounds fresh okra
½ teaspoon salt
½ teaspoon black pepper
½ cup yellow cornmeal
¼ cup grated Parmesan cheese
2 tablespoons flour
¼ cup bacon drippings

•

Wash and trim the okra. Cut into half-inch slices. Place the slices in a bowl and sprinkle with salt and pepper.

In a shallow dish, combine the cornmeal, Parmesan cheese and flour.

Heat the bacon drippings in a skillet over medium heat. Roll the okra slices in the cornmeal mixture and fry on both sides until golden brown. Drain on paper towels and serve with a variety of sauces for dipping.

OKRA SUCCOTASH

serves 4

4 ham hocks
2 pounds string beans
1 onion, sliced then sliced again in half
1 teaspoon salt
8 small new potatoes, peeled
1 cup fresh corn
1 pound okra, trimmed but left whole

•

Simmer the ham hocks in a large pot in enough water to cover for 1 hour.

Wash the beans, break in half and add to the ham hocks at the end of the 1 hour of cooking time. Add the onion and salt, stir, and then add the potatoes. Simmer for 15 minutes. Add the corn and okra to the pot and stir gently. Simmer for 20 minutes. Serve with cornbread.

STEWED OKRA, CREOLE-STYLE

serves 6

2 pounds fresh okra
3 tablespoons butter
1 onion, chopped
1 green bell pepper, chopped
1 red bell pepper, chopped
2 garlic cloves, finely minced
3 tomatoes, chopped
½ teaspoon salt
½ teaspoon black pepper
½ teaspoon cayenne pepper
1 tablespoon chopped parsley

•

Wash and trim the okra, and set aside. Melt the butter in a large skillet and add the onion, green bell pepper, red bell pepper and garlic. Blend well and sauté for 6 minutes. Add the tomatoes, salt, cayenne pepper, pepper and parsley and stir well. Blend in the okra and simmer for 20 minutes over medium-low heat.

CREAMED ONIONS

serves 6

2 pounds small white onions
water
½ teaspoon salt
1 tablespoon butter
1 tablespoon flour
1 cup evaporated milk
1 bay leaf
½ teaspoon salt
½ teaspoon paprika

•

Carefully peel the onions and place them in a skillet with enough water to cover. Add the salt and simmer for 20 minutes or until tender, but do not overcook. While the onions simmer, melt the butter in the top half of a double boiler. Blend in the flour and then stir in the milk. Simmer for 5 minutes. Add the bay leaf and salt and simmer for 5 minutes more. Drain the water from the onions and pour the cream sauce over them. Sprinkle the paprika over the top and serve.

SMOTHERED PARSNIPS

serves 4

8 small parsnips
5 tablespoons butter
1 garlic clove, finely minced
1 tablespoon honey
1 tablespoon fresh chopped parsley

•

Wash, rinse and gently peel the parsnips. Place them in a saucepan with enough cold water to cover and boil in lightly salted water for 1 hour. Drain the parsnips and cool. Slice lengthwise into half-inch thick strips.

Melt the butter in a large skillet and blend in the garlic and honey. Stir in the parsnip strips and sprinkle with the parsley. Cover the skillet and cook over medium heat for 3 minutes. Turn the parsnip strips and cook, covered, for 3 minutes more. Stir and serve.

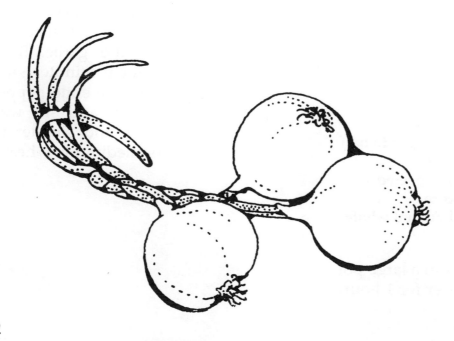

FRESH PEAS

serves 6

2 pounds peas in their pods
3 tablespoons butter
1 onion, sliced and halved
1 small garlic clove, finely chopped
½ teaspoon salt
½ teaspoon black pepper
1 tablespoon lemon juice
¼ teaspoon paprika

•

Shell the peas into a saucepan and add enough cold water to just cover. Bring to a boil and cook rapidly, uncovered, for 20 minutes, or until the peas are just tender. Drain and set aside.

Melt the butter in a skillet over medium heat and sauté the onions. Stir in the garlic, salt, pepper and lemon juice and simmer for 2 minutes. Stir in the peas gently and reduce heat to low. Simmer, stirring occasionally, for 5 minutes. Sprinkle with paprika and serve.

CREAMED POTATOES, PEAS AND PEARL ONIONS

serves 6

1 cup pearl onions
4 large potatoes, cooked, peeled and diced
2 cups fresh peas
¼ cup fresh chopped parsley
1 teaspoon salt
½ teaspoon cayenne pepper
2 tablespoons butter
2 tablespoons sifted flour
1 cup light cream
¼ teaspoon paprika

•

Preheat the oven to 325°F.

Peel the onions and cook them in a pot of boiling water for 4 minutes. Drain well. Combine the potatoes, peas, onions, parsley, salt and cayenne pepper in a bowl and toss. Turn the mixture into a lightly buttered casserole dish.

Melt the butter in a skillet and blend in the flour until smooth. Add the cream and cook over medium heat until it starts to bubble, stirring constantly. Reduce heat and simmer for 5 minutes. Pour the white sauce over the vegetables and sprinkle the paprika over it. Bake, covered, for 20 minutes.

PECAN CASSEROLE

serves 4

3 cups sliced celery
1 tablespoon sugar
1½ cups pecan halves
4 tablespoons butter
3 tablespoons flour
1 cup light cream
1 teaspoon salt
½ teaspoon hot red pepper flakes
1 egg, beaten

•

In a saucepan, combine the celery and sugar. Add enough water to cover completely. Cover the saucepan and bring the mixture to a boil. Lower the heat and cook until the celery is tender, about 12 to 15 minutes. Drain the celery and mix with the pecan halves in a bowl.

Preheat the oven to 325°F.

Melt the butter in a small saucepan. Add the flour and stir until well blended. Cook, stirring constantly, for 2 minutes. Gradually stir in the cream. Continue cooking, stirring, until the mixture is thick. Remove the saucepan from the heat and stir in the salt, red pepper and egg. Add to the celery-pecan mixture and mix well.

Butter a 1 ½-quart casserole or baking dish. Pour the mixture into the casserole and bake for 30 minutes. Serve hot.

BACON AND CHEDDAR TATERS

serves 6

½ pound bacon, diced
4 large unpeeled potatoes, chopped
1 onion, coarsely chopped
1 tablespoon chopped parsley
2 cups shredded cheddar cheese

•

Place the bacon in a skillet and fry until medium-well done. Stir in the potatoes and cook over medium heat, stirring constantly, for 5 minutes. Stir in the onion and parsley and continue to cook over medium heat, stirring constantly, for 10 minutes. Drain off any bacon drippings and stir in the cheese. Continue to cook, stirring, until the cheese has melted. Serve hot.

Heavenly Hash Browns

serves 6

4 large unpeeled potatoes, scrubbed
and shredded
1 onion, finely chopped
8 tablespoons bacon drippings
1 tablespoon chopped fresh parsley
1 teaspoon salt
1 teaspoon black pepper
1½ cups shredded cheddar cheese

•

Mix the potatoes with the onion in a bowl and set aside.

Place 4 tablespoons of the bacon drippings in a skillet over medium heat. Add the potatoes, and pat them down into the skillet with your hand or a spatula. Sprinkle with the parsley, salt and pepper.

Evenly coat a second skillet with the remaining bacon drippings. When the potatoes are golden brown on the side down, loosen them all the way around the inside edge of the skillet and the bottom with a spatula. Flip the potatoes into the second skillet, top with the cheese and cook until the bottom is golden.

Home Fries

serves 6

4 large unpeeled potatoes, coarsely
chopped
1 large onion, coarsely chopped
1 large green bell pepper, coarsely
chopped
1 tablespoon chopped parsley
1 teaspoon salt
½ teaspoon cayenne pepper
5 tablespoons butter

•

Combine the potatoes, onion, green bell pepper, parsley, salt and cayenne pepper in a mixing bowl and toss well.

Melt the butter in a large skillet over medium heat. Stir in the potato mixture and continue stirring as you cook the mixture for 15 minutes. Serve hot.

POTATO HOE CAKE

serves 6

**2 large potatoes, peeled and coarsely
grated
1 cup cornmeal
1 teaspoon salt
1 cup milk
bacon drippings for frying
6 butter pats**

•

Combine the potatoes, cornmeal and salt in a large mixing bowl and mix well. Heat the milk in a saucepan and bring to a boil.

Pour the milk over the mixture and blend thoroughly.

Heat a half-inch layer of bacon drippings in a deep skillet over medium heat. Pour the mixture into the skillet as you would a pancake to make 6 cakes. Each cake should be a half-inch thick. Fry until golden brown, place a slice of butter on each cake and flip. Fry on second side until golden brown and drain on paper towels. Serve with apple sauce, ketchup or sour cream.

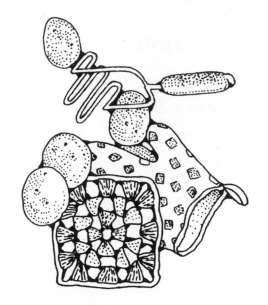

POTATO CHIPS

serves a bunch

**10 large potatoes, peeled
1 cup olive oil
1 cup vegetable oil
1 tablespoon garlic powder
1 tablespoon salt
1 tablespoon finely chopped fresh
parsley**

•

Use a potato peeler or vegetable slicer to slice the potatoes paper thin. Place the slices in a large bowl and cover with cold water. Soak for 2 hours, drain and carefully pat dry with paper towels.

Combine the oils, garlic powder, salt and parsley in a bowl and blend thoroughly. Pour the mixture into a deep skillet and heat to 300°F. Fry the chips, one handful at a time, until golden in color. Drain on paper towels.

BAKED RICE RING

serves 6

1 cup cooked rice
3 onions, chopped
¼ cup butter
½ pound mushrooms, thinly sliced
½ teaspoon salt
½ teaspoon black pepper
2 tablespoons fresh chopped parsley

•

Preheat the oven to 350°F. Melt the butter in a skillet. Add the onions and sauté for 5 minutes. Add the mushrooms, salt and pepper and sauté for 8 minutes. Combine the rice, onions, mushrooms and parsley and mix well. Turn the mixture into a buttered circular mold, and bake for 30 minutes.

BROWN RICE 'N' STUFF

serves 6

3½ cups water
1½ teaspoons salt
1½ cups brown rice
4 tablespoons butter
2 onions, finely chopped
2 green bell peppers, chopped
4 celery stalks with leaves, finely chopped
1 garlic clove, finely minced
½ pound chicken giblets, chopped
½ teaspoon hot red-pepper sauce
½ teaspoon Worcestershire sauce
½ teaspoon salt
½ teaspoon black pepper
½ teaspoon cayenne pepper

•

Bring the water and salt to a boil and add the rice. Lower the heat and simmer, covered, for 45 minutes, or until all the water is absorbed. While the rice is cooking, melt the butter in a skillet. Add the onions, green bell pepper, celery and garlic and simmer for 20 minutes. Stir in the chicken giblets, hot red-pepper sauce, Worcestershire sauce, salt, pepper and cayenne pepper and simmer for 10 minutes.

When the rice is cooked, add it to the skillet and heat for 5 minutes, stirring constantly.

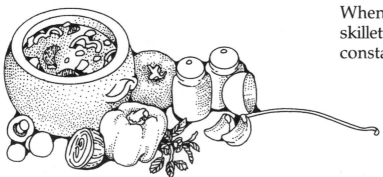

ROAST POTATOES

serves 6

6 medium potatoes, peeled
1 large onion, sliced and pushed into
rings
½ cup olive oil
1 tablespoon Worcestershire sauce
2 tablespoons chopped parsley
1 teaspoon salt
½ teaspoon black pepper
½ teaspoon paprika

•

Cut the potatoes into thick wedges and mix in a large bowl with the onions. Preheat the oven to 350°F. Combine the olive oil, Worcestershire sauce, parsley, salt, pepper and paprika in a bowl and blend well. Pour the oil mixture over the potatoes and onion and toss to coat thoroughly. Turn mixture into a casserole or baking dish and bake for 35 to 45 minutes, stirring occasionally.

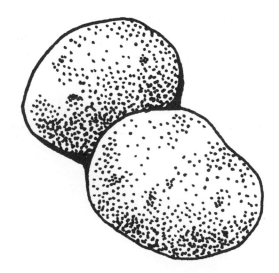

DEEP-FRIED RICE BALLS

serves 6

½ package active dry yeast
½ cup *very* warm water
1½ cups very soft cooked rice
3 eggs, beaten
1¼ cups flour, sifted
¼ cup sugar
½ teaspoon salt
¼ teaspoon nutmeg
¼ cup confectioners' sugar
vegetable oil for frying

•

Place the warm water in a bowl and sprinkle in the yeast. Let stand for several minutes and then stir until well dissolved. Mash the cooked rice in a bowl and allow to stand until cool. Stir the yeast mixture into the rice and allow to rise overnight, covered.

Add the eggs, flour, sugar, salt and nutmeg to the mixture and beat until smooth.

Allow the mixture to stand for 30 minutes.

Sprinkle a little flour over a cutting board, spoon out the rice mixture and roll into balls.

Fill a large, deep skillet with oil to a depth of 2 inches. Heat until very hot.

Deep-fry the balls for 3 minutes, and drain on paper towels. Dust with confectioners' sugar and serve warm.

DIRTY RICE

serves 6 to 8

1½ cups brown rice
3½ cups water
1½ teaspoons salt
2 onions, finely chopped
2 green peppers, finely chopped
4 celery stalks, with leaves, finely chopped
1 garlic clove, finely chopped
2 tablespoons bacon drippings
½ pound chicken giblets, chopped
Tabasco sauce to taste
Worcestershire sauce to taste
salt to taste
black pepper to taste
cayenne pepper to taste

•

Bring the water and salt to a boil in a medium saucepan. Add the rice, cover tightly, and lower the heat. Cook for 50 minutes or until all the water is absorbed. Set the rice aside.

Heat the bacon drippings in a skillet. Add the onions, peppers, celery and garlic. Sauté, stirring often, for 30 minutes or until most of the liquid is gone.

Add the chopped chicken giblets (gizzards, livers, and hearts) and sauté until they are browned. Add the Tabasco sauce, Worcestershire sauce, salt, cayenne pepper and pepper to taste. Mix in the rice. Combine well and heat thoroughly. Serve hot.

HOPPIN' JOHN

serves 6

1 cup dried black-eyed peas
water
1 teaspoon salt
1 onion, diced
2 ounces salt pork, diced
½ teaspoon black pepper
¼ teaspoon cayenne pepper
1 cup raw long-grained rice
1 tablespoon butter

•

Rinse the peas well and place in a bowl with 3 cups cold water; soak for 8 hours. Drain the peas and reserve the liquid. Add enough water to make a total of 3 cups. Place the water, black-eyed peas, salt, onion and salt pork in a large pot and bring to a boil. Lower the heat and add the pepper, cayenne pepper, rice and butter to the pot. Stir and simmer, covered, for 25 minutes.

NUTTY RICE

serves 6

3 tablespoons butter
1 teaspoon oregano
1½ cups raw rice
¼ cup slivered almonds
¼ cup pine nuts
2½ cups water
1 teaspoon salt
¼ teaspoon hot red-pepper sauce

•

Melt the butter in a large skillet and stir in the oregano, rice, almonds and pine nuts. Sauté for 3 minutes over medium heat. Add the water and salt and bring the mixture to a boil.

Reduce the heat and simmer, covered, for 25 minutes or until all liquid is absorbed.

RICE PILAU

serves 4

6 bacon slices, coarsely chopped
1 onion, chopped
1 celery stalk, chopped
2 cups stewed tomatoes
1½ cups hot water
2 teaspoons salt
½ teaspoon black pepper
1 cup raw rice

•

Cook the bacon well in a skillet, remove with a slotted spoon and drain on paper towels. Set aside.

Add the onion and celery to the bacon drippings and cook over medium heat until tender. Combine the tomatoes, hot water, salt and pepper with the celery and onion and stir well. Bring to a boil and slowly add the rice. Reduce heat, cover and simmer for 20 minutes or until the liquid is absorbed.

RICE FRITTERS

serves 6

2 eggs, separated
1 cup sugar
1 cup cooked rice
2 cups flour, sifted
2 teaspoons baking powder
vegetable oil for frying

•

In a large mixing bowl, combine the egg yolks, sugar, rice, flour and baking powder. Blend well.

Beat the egg whites in another bowl until they are stiff. Fold into the rice mixture. Blend well.

Fill a large, deep skillet with oil to a depth of 1 inch. Heat until very hot. Drop the batter into the oil by the teaspoonful and cook 3 minutes or until golden brown. Serve with sauces for dipping, or dust with confectioners' sugar.

RED RICE

serves 6

4 bacon slices
2 onions, chopped
6 ounces tomato paste
1½ cups water
1 tablespoon salt
½ teaspoon black pepper
1 tablespoon sugar
2 cups raw rice

•

Fry the bacon in a skillet until crisp. Drain the bacon on paper towels and set aside. Drain off ½ cup bacon drippings and reserve. Add the onions to the skillet and sauté for 5 minutes. Add the tomato paste and water, blend thoroughly and simmer over low heat for 10 minutes. Add the salt, pepper, sugar, rice and reserved bacon drippings. Cover and simmer over low heat for 30 minutes. Crumble in the bacon and continue to cook for 30 minutes more.

SPINACH AND RICE

serves 6

3 cups water
1 tablespoon salt
½ teaspoon black pepper
½ teaspoon cayenne pepper
1½ pounds fresh spinach, well rinsed
and coarsely chopped
1 cup stewed tomatoes
2 cups raw rice
1 teaspoon sugar

•

Bring the water and the salt to a boil in a large pot.

Add the pepper, cayenne pepper, spinach, tomatoes and sugar and bring back to a boil. Stir in the rice, lower the heat and simmer for 25 minutes, or until the water is absorbed.

FRIED ACORN SQUASH

serves 6

4 large peeled acorn squash
2 eggs, beaten
¼ teaspoon nutmeg
½ teaspoon cinnamon
¾ cup cracker meal
1 cup vegetable oil

•

Slice the squash into half-inch rings. Remove the seeds and fiber, and soak in lightly salted water for 20 minutes. Drain and pat dry.

Add the nutmeg and cinnamon to the beaten eggs and blend well.

Heat the oil in a deep skillet. Dip the squash into the egg mixture and then into the cracker meal. Cook on both sides until golden. Drain on paper towels before serving.

SUMMER SQUASH

serves 6

6 medium summer (yellow) squash, thinly sliced
1 large onion, thinly sliced
6 butter pats
1 teaspoon oregano
½ teaspoon salt
½ teaspoon black pepper
4 tablespoons lemon juice
½ cup white wine
½ teaspoon paprika

•

Arrange the squash and onion in alternative layers in a large skillet. Cover the vegetables with the 6 pats of butter. Sprinkle with the oregano, salt and pepper. Sprinkle with the lemon juice and carefully add the wine.

Sprinkle with the paprika, cover the skillet and cook over medium-low heat for 30 minutes.

SOUTH CAROLINA DRY RICE

serves 4

1 cup raw long-grained rice
1½ cups water
1 teaspoon salt
1 tablespoon lemon juice
2 tablespoons butter

•

Combine all the ingredients in a large skillet and bring to a boil. Stir once with a fork and cover. Lower the heat and simmer for 20 minutes, or until all the water is absorbed.

STUFFED ACORN SQUASH

serves 4

4 small acorn squash
1 teaspoon salt
3 eggs
2 tablespoons grated onion
1½ cups grated cheddar cheese
4 tablespoons fine, unflavored
breadcrumbs
½ teaspoon salt
½ teaspoon black pepper
8 thin butter pats

•

Preheat the oven to 350°F. Cook the squash in a large pot of boiling salted water until almost tender, about 20 minutes. Drain and remove the tops so as to leave a cavity for filling. Scoop out the seeds and fiber and pour out any water that has collected. Put the squash in a lightly buttered baking pan, cavity-side up.

Beat the eggs in a bowl until frothy. Add the onion, cheese, breadcrumbs, salt and pepper. Fill each squash with one-fourth of the mixture and top with 2 butter pats. Bake for 30 minutes and serve.

SQUASH AND CORN PUDDING

serves 6

1 pound summer squash, thinly sliced
1 onion, thinly sliced
1 egg
½ cup corn
½ cup heavy cream
½ teaspoon baking powder
½ cup unflavored breadcrumbs
½ cup grated cheddar cheese
salt to taste
black pepper to taste
butter

•

Cook the squash and onion over very high heat in a covered pot filled to a depth of 2 inches with water. When the squash and onion are very soft, drain them well and put them into a mixing bowl and mash them together.

Stir in the corn, cream, baking powder, breadcrumbs, grated cheese, salt and pepper. Mix well to blend all the ingredients evenly together.

Preheat the oven to 350°F.

Pour the squash and corn mixture into a greased casserole dish. Dot the top of the pudding all over with butter and bake for 1 hour, or until the pudding is golden brown.

Serve hot, with some melted butter drizzled over the top of each portion.

BRANDIED SWEET POTATO MASH

serves 6

4 cups hot mashed sweet potatoes
4 tablespoons softened butter
¼ cup sugar
¼ teaspoon ground ginger
¼ teaspoon nutmeg
¼ teaspoon cinnamon
1 teaspoon salt
¼ cup brandy
2 tablespoons light cream

●

Preheat the oven to 375°F. Combine the potatoes, butter, sugar, ginger, nutmeg, cinnamon and salt in a large mixing bowl and blend thoroughly. Stir in the brandy and cream and blend thoroughly. Turn the mixture into a well-buttered casserole and bake, uncovered, for 30 minutes.

CANDIED SWEET POTATOES

serves 6

6 medium yams or sweet potatoes
¼ cup brown sugar
1 teaspoon grated lemon peel
2 tablespoons sifted flour
¼ teaspoon salt
¼ teaspoon cinnamon
¼ teaspoon nutmeg
3 tablespoons butter, broken into small pieces
1 cup orange juice

●

Place the yams in a large pot and cover with water. Bring to a rapid boil and cook for 15 minutes. Run cold water over the yams.

While the yams cool, combine the sugar, lemon peel, flour, salt, cinnamon and nutmeg in a small bowl. Blend well.

Preheat the oven to 350°F.

When the yams are cool enough to handle, remove them from the water, pat dry and slice in half lengthwise. Remove the skins. Slice the yams.

In a well-buttered casserole make a layer of half the yams. Sprinkle with half the orange juice and then half the spice mixture. Dot with half the butter. Repeat with the remaining ingredients. Bake, uncovered, for 45 minutes. Cool slightly before serving.

Glazed Sweet Potatoes and Apple Casserole

serves 6

4 medium sweet potatoes or yams
2 large apples, peeled, cored and sliced
2 teaspoons lemon juice
½ teaspoon salt
4 tablespoons butter
⅓ cup molasses
¼ cup packed brown sugar
¼ cup chopped walnuts

•

Place the sweet potatoes in a pot and cover with water. Bring to a rapid boil and cook for 15 minutes. Place the pot under cold running water and allow the sweet potatoes to cool.

Spinkle the apples with the lemon juice and salt. When the sweet potatoes are cool enough to handle, pat dry and slice in half lengthwise. Remove the skins. Slice the sweet potatoes and arrange the slices in a shallow baking dish.

Preheat the oven to 325°F.

Melt the butter in a skillet and add the apple slices. Stir constantly, but gently, for 2 minutes. Remove the apples with a slotted spoon and arrange over the sweet potato slices. Add the molasses to the remaining butter in the skillet and bring to a Boil. Pour the molasses over the sweet potatoes and apples. Sprinkle with brown sugar and walnuts and bake for 30 minutes.

Sweet Potato Croquettes

serves 6

3 cups mashed sweet potatoes
1 teaspoon salt
½ teaspoon cayenne pepper
3 tablespoons light cream
¾ cup finely chopped walnuts
1 egg, slightly beaten
5 tablespoons cracker meal
vegetable oil for frying

•

Combine the mashed potatoes, salt, cayenne pepper, cream and nuts and blend well.

Fill a skillet to a depth of one-half inch with oil. Heat over medium heat. Shape the sweet potato mixture into small croquettes. Dip them in the egg, and then roll them in the cracker meal.

Fry until golden brown and drain on paper towels.

SWEET POTATO PIE

serves 6

3 medium sweet potatoes (yams)
3 large eggs
1¼ cups sugar
¼ teaspoon salt
½ teaspoon ground allspice
1 teaspoon cinnamon
¼ teaspoon nutmeg
1 cup heavy cream
1 unbaked 9-inch pie shell

●

Place the sweet potatoes in a large pot and cover with water. Bring to a rapid boil and cook for 1 hour.

Preheat the oven to 350°F.

Just before the sweet potatoes are ready, combine the eggs, salt, all-spice, cinnamon, nutmeg and cream in a blender. Process on low speed for 2 minutes. Run cold water on the sweet potatoes for several minutes. When the potatoes are cool enough to handle, slice them in half length-wise and lay them on a cutting board, meat-side down. Remove the skins, cut off the stem ends if they are tough or fibrous. Cut the sweet potatoes into chunks. Drop one chunk at a time into the blender, and process, making sure that each chunk is well blended. Pour the mixture into the pie shell and bake for 1 hour. Cool slightly and serve warm, or refrigerate and top with whipped cream before serving.

SWEET POTATO PONE

serves 8

4 large, uncooked sweet potatoes
2 eggs
½ cup brown sugar
½ cup canned crushed pineapple, well-drained
grated rind of 1 lemon
grated rind of 1 large orange
1 teaspoon cinnamon
½ teaspoon nutmeg
½ cup dark molasses
1 teaspoon ground cloves
1 cup light cream
½ cup sweet butter

●

Peel the sweet potatoes and grate them finely.

In a mixing bowl, beat the eggs. Gradually add the sugar, beating constantly. Stir in the pineapple, sweet potatoes, lemon rind, orange rind, cinnamon, nutmeg, molasses, cloves, cream and butter. Beat until thoroughly blended.

Pour the mixture into a buttered baking dish. Bake for 1 hour, or until browned on top. Serve hot, topped with a little more grated orange peel.

Sweet Potato Pudding

serves 6

3 cups mashed sweet potatoes
3 tablespoons softened butter
1 teaspoon salt
½ teaspoon black pepper
¼ teaspoon cinnamon
1 egg, beaten
3 tablespoons brown sugar
1 cup grated, unsweetened coconut
¼ cup coconut milk

•

Preheat the oven to 350°F. Combine the sweet potatoes, butter, salt, pepper, cinnamon, egg, sugar, coconut and coconut milk in a mixing bowl and blend thoroughly. Turn into a buttered casserole dish and bake, uncovered, for 30 minutes.

Glazed Turnips

serves 6

2 pounds white turnips, peeled and sliced
7 tablespoons butter
1 tablespoon honey
1 teaspoon sugar
½ teaspoon grated nutmeg

•

Melt the butter in a large skillet and blend in the honey. Stir in the turnips and cook over medium heat for 3 minutes, stirring constantly. Combine the sugar and nutmeg and sprinkle over the turnips. Cover the dish and simmer over low heat for 10 minutes. Stir and serve.

Mashed Turnips and Carrots

serves 6

1 large yellow turnip
6 large carrots
¾ stick butter
1 onion, diced
2 tablespoons sugar
2 teaspoons salt

•

Peel and quarter the turnip. Pare and halve the carrots. Place the vegetables in a saucepan and cover with water. Boil rapidly for 25 minutes or until very tender. Drain the vegetables and place them in a large bowl.

Mash the vegetables with a potato masher. In a skillet melt the butter and sauté the onions. Stir in the sugar and salt and simmer for 2 minutes. Stir in the vegetables and simmer for 3 minutes, stirring constantly.

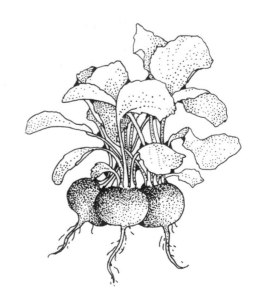

VEGETABLE CASSEROLE

serves 12

1 cup thinly sliced carrots
1 cup fresh green beans, trimmed and halved
1 cup peeled, diced white potatoes
½ cup chopped celery
2 tomatoes, quartered
1 yellow squash, sliced
½ small cauliflower, broken into flowerets
1 small onion, chopped
1 red bell pepper, chopped
½ cup fresh peas
½ cup beef bouillon
⅓ cup olive oil
2 garlic cloves, minced
1 bay leaf
2 teaspoons salt
1 teaspoon chopped fresh dill
½ teaspoon oregano

•

Preheat the oven to 350°F. Combine the vegetables in a large mixing bowl and turn into a large, un-greased casserole dish.

Combine the beef bouillon, olive oil, garlic, bay leaf, salt, dill and oregano in a saucepan and bring to a boil. Remove the bay leaf and pour the sauce over the vegetables. Bake, covered, for 1 hour, stirring every 15 minutes.

SAUTÉED VEGETABLES

serves 6

2 tablespoons butter
2 tablespoons olive oil
1 large onion, sliced and pushed into rings
1 small eggplant, thinly sliced and quartered
1 medium yellow squash, sliced
1 zucchini, sliced
1 green bell pepper, julienned
2 green tomatoes, chopped
1 red tomato, chopped
½ teaspoon dried savory
½ teaspoon salt
½ teaspoon black pepper
1 tablespoon lemon juice

•

In a large skillet melt the butter and blend in the olive oil. Add the onion and sauté until tender. Add the egg-plant, yellow squash, zucchini, green bell pepper, green tomatoes, red tomato, salt, pepper and lemon juice.

Toss well. Sauté over low heat, stirring constantly, but gently, until all the vegetables are tender.

Split Pea Soup

Shrimp and Avocado Cocktail
(overleaf)

Southern-Style Potato Salad

SEAFOOD

GRILLED BASS WITH HERBS

serves 6

6 8-ounce bass fillets
1 cup white wine or dry vermouth
⅓ cup olive oil
1 cup chopped fresh mushrooms
½ cup chopped scallions
2 tablespoons lemon juice
2 teaspoons salt
¼ teaspoon cayenne pepper
¼ teaspoon dried tarragon

•

Heat the coals in a barbecue until they are gray and very hot.

Cut 6 pieces of heavy aluminum foil or (doubled regular aluminum foil) into 18-inch squares. Lightly oil the foil.

In a large bowl combine the wine, olive oil, mushrooms, scallions, lemon juice, salt, pepper and tarragon. Mix well.

Place one fillet on each piece of foil. Pour the dressing over the pieces. Wrap the fish in the foil and seal carefully. Place the packages on the grill, about 6 inches from the coals.

Grill for 20 to 25 minutes or until the fish flakes easily when tested with a fork. Serve hot.

OVEN-FRIED SHERRY CATFISH

serves 6

6 8-ounce catfish fillets
1 cup soft unflavored breadcrumbs
1 tablespoon finely chopped parsley
1 teaspoon paprika
1 teaspoon lemon juice
½ teaspoon white pepper
salt to taste
¼ cup olive oil
1 cup dry sherry
2 lemons, quartered

•

Wash and dry the catfish fillets and set aside. Preheat the oven to 450°F. Grease a baking dish large enough to hold the fillets in one layer.

Put the breadcrumbs into a baking dish and toast them in the oven for 1 minute.

On a plate, combine the breadcrumbs with the parsley, paprika, lemon juice, white pepper and salt to taste. Pour the olive oil into one shallow bowl and the sherry into another. Rub the fillets with the olive oil, then dip them into the sherry. Next roll them in the breadcrumb mixture. Arrange the fillets in the baking dish.

Bake the fish for 10 minutes on each side, sprinkling the fillets with some of the sherry every few minutes.

Serve garnished with the lemon quarters.

CATFISH FRY

serves 4

2 pounds catfish fillets
½ cup flour
¼ cup cornmeal
¼ cup grated Parmesan cheese
1 teaspoon oregano
½ teaspoon cayenne pepper
black pepper to taste
1 egg
2 tablespoons water
salt to taste
½ cup olive oil

•

Wash and dry the fillets.

In a shallow bowl mix the flour, cornmeal, Parmesan cheese, oregano, cayenne pepper and salt and pepper to taste. Set aside.

In another shallow bowl beat the egg and water together.

In a large skillet, heat the olive oil. While waiting for the oil to bubble, dip the fillets in the egg mixture and roll them in the flour mixture until they are well coated. Put the fillets into the skillet and cook for 8 minutes on each side. Remove from the skillet and drain well on paper towels. Serve accompanied by tartar sauce and lemon quarters.

CLAM FRITTERS

serves 4

2 cups finely chopped clams
2 egg yolks
1 cup fine unflavored breadcrumbs
1 tablespoon finely chopped chives
salt to taste
2 egg whites
black pepper to taste
⅓ cup milk
½ cup olive oil

•

Beat the egg whites in a bowl until they are stiff.

In a mixing bowl beat the egg yolks until they are thick. Add the clams, breadcrumbs, chives, salt and pepper. Mix well. Stir in the milk. Fold in the egg whites.

Heat the olive oil in a heavy deep skillet over medium heat. Carefully drop the clam batter by teaspoons into the oil. Do not crowd the skillet. Cook, turning once, until the fritters are browned on both sides, about 5 minutes.

Drain the fritters on paper towels. Transfer to a serving platter and serve hot with lemon wedges.

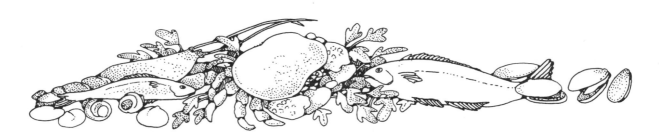

SOUTHERN-STYLE FRIED CATFISH

serves 4

**2 pounds catfish fillets
salt to taste
black pepper to taste
¼ cup bacon drippings
3 tablespoons lemon juice
4 tablespoons chopped parsley
1 teaspoon paprika**

•

Wash and dry the fish and season with salt and pepper.

In a large skillet, heat the bacon drippings. When the drippings are hot, put the fish into the skillet and cook over medium heat for 8 minutes on each side.

Drain the fish on paper towels. Sprinkle with the lemon juice, parsley and paprika. Serve immediately.

CRAB CASSEROLE

serves 4

**3 pounds crab legs
8 tablespoons butter
1½ cups coarse cracker crumbs
2 large onions, finely chopped
6 celery stalks, finely chopped
2 tablespoons finely chopped parsley
¼ cup heavy cream
¼ teaspoon cayenne pepper
1½ teaspoons dry mustard**

•

Rinse the crab legs. Put them into a steamer basket and steam them over boiling water for 10 minutes. Drain the crab legs, shell them and remove any cartilage from the meat. Break up the crabmeat and put it into a large bowl.

Preheat the oven to 350°F. Grease a medium-sized casserole dish with butter.

In a small saucepan, melt the butter over low heat. Remove the pan from the heat and set aside to cool.

Add the cracker crumbs to the crabmeat and mix well. Then add the onion, celery and parsley. Mix well.

In a small bowl, combine the cooled melted butter, the cream, cayenne pepper and dry mustard. Mix thoroughly.

Add the cream mixture to the crab mixture and mix well. Carefully spoon the mixture into the casserole dish. Bake for 30 minutes. Serve immediately.

CRAB LEGS CREOLE

serves 4

12 large crab legs
salt to taste
black pepper to taste
2 cups milk
4 tablespoons flour
8 tablespoons butter
2 garlic cloves, finely chopped
1 teaspoon oregano
2 tablespoons finely chopped parsley
1 teaspoon paprika
2 lemons, quartered

●

Shell the crab legs and remove the cartilage from the meat. Wash the legs and dry them thoroughly. Set aside.

In a large shallow bowl combine ¼ teaspoon salt, ¼ teaspoon pepper and the milk. Put the flour in another large, shallow bowl. Put the crab legs into the milk and soak them for 30 minutes.

A few minutes before the crab legs have finished soaking, melt the butter in a small saucepan. Add the garlic and oregano and mix well. Remove the pan from the heat and set aside.

Take the crab legs, one by one, from the milk and pat them lightly with the flour. Put the crab legs on a rack in the broiler pan. Turn on the broiler. Brush each leg with some of the butter mixture then broil the crab legs for 15 minutes. Turn the legs carefully and broil the other side for 7 minutes.

Carefully transfer the crab legs to a serving platter. Pour the remaining butter mixture over them and sprinkle with parsley and paprika. Garnish with the lemon quarters and serve.

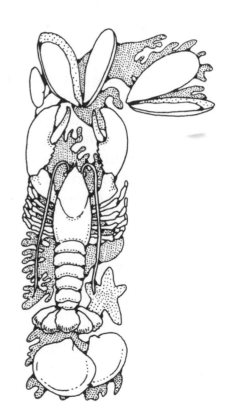

*OIL IN HALF & HOTTER
ONIONS IN HALF
MORE PEPPER*

CRAB CAKES

serves 6

2 pounds crab legs/*LUMP MEAT*
4 tablespoons butter
2 medium-sized onions, finely chopped
1 cup soft <u>unflavored</u> breadcrumbs
3 eggs, beaten
1 teaspoon dry mustard
1 teaspoon Worcestershire sauce
salt
2 tablespoons light cream *?*
½ cup flour
1 cup olive oil
3 lemons, quartered

•

In a large pot bring 2 quarts of water to a boil over high heat. Add the crab legs. When the water returns to a boil, reduce the heat. Simmer the legs for 15 minutes. Drain the crab legs, shell them, and remove the cartilage. Flake the meat into a large bowl.

In a large skillet, melt the butter. Add the onions and cook over low heat until they are soft but not brown. Pour the contents of the skillet over the crab meat. Add the breadcrumbs and mix thoroughly.

In a small bowl beat the eggs. Add the mustard, Worcestershire sauce, and salt to taste. Mix well and add to the crab mixture. Then add the light cream and mix thoroughly.

Shape the crab mixture into 12 cakes. Put the flour on a plate. Dredge the cakes in the flour.

Heat the olive oil in a large skillet. When the oil is hot, add the cakes. Fry until they are golden brown,

about 3 minutes. Carefully turn the crab cakes and cook on the other side. Serve with the lemon quarters.

FRIED CRAB LEGS

serves 6

18 crab legs
2 eggs
2 tablespoons milk
4 tablespoons flour
4 tablespoons cracker meal
4 tablespoons grated Parmesan cheese
12 tablespoons butter
2 garlic cloves, finely chopped
1 tablespoon lemon juice
1 teaspoon oregano

•

Shell the crab legs and remove the cartilage from the meat. Wash thoroughly. Put the crabmeat on a clean kitchen towel to dry.

In a small mixing bowl, beat the eggs. Add the milk and mix well.

In a large, shallow bowl, combine the flour, cracker meal and Parmesan cheese. Dip the crab legs first in the egg mixture, then dredge them in the flour mixture. Shake off any excess flour.

In a large skillet, over low heat, melt half the butter. Put the crab legs into the skillet, increase the heat to medium, and fry until they are browned and crisp on the edges. Turn and fry the other side.

While the crab legs are cooking, melt the remaining butter in a small saucepan. Add the garlic, lemon juice and oregano.

Drain the crab legs on paper towels. Transfer them to a serving platter and serve immediately with the butter mixture in a dish on the side for dipping.

SOFT-SHELL CRABS À LA CREOLE

serves 6

12 soft-shell crabs
2 cups milk
4 tablespoons flour
½ cup melted butter
salt to taste
black pepper to taste
2 lemons, quartered
parsley sprigs

•

Clean the crabs and rinse them well in cold water. Dry with a clean towel and season generously with salt and pepper.

Season the milk with salt and pepper. Place the crabs in the milk and soak them for 30 minutes.

Remove the crabs from the milk and pat them lightly with the flour. Shake off any excess. Brush each crab with melted butter.

Preheat the broiler.

Place the crabs on a rack set in a broiler pan. Broil until the crabs are a delicate brown, about 15 minutes. Turn the crabs over after about 7 minutes.

Serve on a platter garnished with lemon quarters and parsley. Pour a little melted butter and chopped parsley over the crabs. Serve hot.

CRAB SOUFFLÉS

serves 6

2 pounds crab legs
2 tablespoons butter
2 tablespoons flour
salt to taste
black pepper to taste
1 cup milk
2 eggs, separated
1 cup heavy cream, whipped

•

Shell the crab legs and remove the cartilage from the meat. Wash and dry the crabmeat, then break it up and put it into a large mixing bowl. Preheat the oven to 350°F. Butter six individual soufflé dishes.

In a saucepan, melt the butter over low heat. Add the flour, and salt and pepper to taste. Blend well. Gradually add the milk, stirring constantly. Cook until the mixture thickens, then remove the pan from the heat.

In a large mixing bowl, beat the egg yolks. Stirring constantly, slowly add the butter mixture to the yolks. Add the crabmeat to the mixture, then fold in the whipped cream. In a separate bowl, beat the egg whites until they are stiff. Fold the egg whites into the crab mixture.

Divide the mixture among the six individual soufflé dishes. Set the dishes in a large baking pan. Add water to the pan so that it comes halfway up the sides of the soufflé dishes. Bake for 40 minutes, or until the soufflés are firm. Serve immediately.

BOILED CRAWFISH

serves 6

50 crawfish (crayfish)
1 garlic clove, chopped
1 teaspoon whole allspice
6 whole cloves
2 quarts white wine
3 tablespoons salt
1 teaspoon cayenne pepper
3 bay leaves
1 teaspoon hot red-pepper sauce

•

Wash and drain the crawfish. Set aside. Put the garlic, allspice and cloves on a small square of cheesecloth and tie closed with a piece of string to make a little pouch.

Bring 2 quarts water to a boil in a very large pot. Add the herb pouch and continue to boil for 5 minutes.

Add the wine, salt, cayenne pepper, bay leaves, hot red-pepper sauce and the crawfish and bring the liquid back to a boil. Cook for 20 minutes or until the crawfish are bright red.

Remove the pot from the heat and let the crawfish cool in their liquid for 30 minutes. Drain the crawfish and serve with hot sauce.

FRIED MUSSELS PARMESAN

serves 4

48 mussels, about 4 pounds, scrubbed and debearded
2 eggs
2 tablespoons cold water
4 tablespoons unflavored breadcrumbs
1 teaspoon garlic powder
4 tablespoons grated Parmesan cheese
1 cup olive oil

•

Put the mussels into a steamer basket and steam them over boiling water until the shells open, about 6 minutes. Discard any mussels that do not open.

Remove the mussels from the shells and discard the shells. Dry the mussels on paper towels.

In a small bowl beat the eggs and cold water together. On a plate mix together the breadcrumbs, garlic powder and Parmesan cheese.

Dip the mussels into the egg mixture and then roll them in the breadcrumb mixture.

Heat the olive oil in a skillet over medium heat until it is very hot. Add the mussels and fry them until they are golden brown. Drain on paper towels and serve hot.

POMPANO À LA MAITRE D'HÔTEL

serves 4

1 4-pound pompano or 2 2-pound
pompanos
1 tablespoon olive oil
1 tablespoon butter
2 tablespoons lemon juice
1 lemon, sliced
salt to taste
black pepper to taste
parsley sprigs for garnish

MAITRE D'HÔTEL SAUCE:
1 tablespoon butter
1 tablespoon flour
1 tablespoon lemon juice
1 tablespoon chopped parsley
2 cups fish stock, chicken broth or
water
1 egg yolk, beaten

•

Preheat the broiler.

Clean the fish. If the fish are large, split them down the back; if they are small, broil them whole.

Season the fish with salt, pepper and olive oil.

Put the fish in a broiler pan and broil until well browned, about 10 to 12 minutes per side. Turn the fish once.

When done, remove the fish to a heated serving platter and dot with the butter. Sprinkle them with the lemon juice.

To make the maitre d'hôtel sauce, place the butter and flour in a saucepan. Heat and stir until well blended. Do not burn. Continue mixing over low heat and add the fish stock, chicken broth or water. Stir well. Add the lemon juice and chopped parsley. Bring the sauce to a boil and cook for about 15 minutes, or until the sauce is reduced by about half. Remove the sauce from the heat and stir in the beaten egg yolk. Mix until well blended. Serve with the broiled fish.

DEEP-FRIED PORGY

serves 4

3 pounds porgy or butterfish fillets,
unskinned
2 teaspoons salt
½ teaspoon black pepper
1 cup yellow cornmeal
lard or oil for deep frying

•

Wash and dry the fillets. Score them on the fleshy side with a sharp knife, making approximately 3 small slashes per fillet.

Season the fillets well with salt and pepper on both sides. Dip them into the cornmeal. Make sure the fillets are coated evenly. Gently shake off the excess cornmeal.

In a large deep skillet heat a ½-inch layer of oil or lard. When it is very hot, add the fish. Fry for 4 minutes on the first side. Turn the fillets carefully and fry for 3 to 4 minutes longer or until they are golden brown. Drain the fillets well on paper towels and serve hot.

STUFFED POMPANO

serves 4

4 small whole pompanos
1 pound cooked shrimp, shelled and deveined
1 egg, well beaten
½ teaspoon salt
¼ teaspoon black pepper
⅛ teaspoon cayenne pepper
3 tablespoons sherry
1 cup light cream

●

Preheat the oven to 350°F.

Clean and wash the fish. Split the fish, leaving the heads and tails intact.

Place the fish in a greased, shallow baking· dish. The dish should be large enough to hold all the fish in one layer.

Chop the shrimp finely. In a small bowl, combine the shrimp, egg, salt, black pepper, cayenne pepper, sherry and ½ cup of the light cream.

Stuff the cavities of the fish with the shrimp mixture. Pour the remaining cream over the fish and bake for 40 minutes. Baste occasionally. Serve the fish hot with the pan juices.

BAKED REDFISH

serves 4

1 4-pound redfish
3 to 4 tablespoons butter
salt to taste
cayenne pepper to taste
6 shrimps, cooked and coarsely chopped
¼ cup chopped capers
lemon wedges for garnish

●

Preheat the oven to 400°F.

Clean and wash the fish. Pat dry.

Place 2 tablespoons of butter, cut up into small pieces, inside the fish. Dot the outside of the fish with the remaining butter. Season the fish to taste with salt and cayenne pepper.

Place the fish in a well-buttered shallow baking dish. Cover it with a piece of well-buttered brown paper or aluminum foil cut to fit. Bake for 40 minutes or until the fish flakes easily with a fork.

Five minutes before the fish is ready, remove it from the oven. Sprinkle the capers and shrimp around the fish. Return to the oven for 5 minutes.

Serve surrounded with the shrimp and capers and garnished with lemon wedges.

BLACKENED REDFISH

serves 8

8 8-ounce skinned redfish or any other
firm white fish fillets
2 cups sweet butter
¼ cup lemon juice
1 tablespoon dried thyme
2 teaspoons black pepper
1½ teaspoons cayenne pepper
1 teaspoon salt

•

Remove any small bones from the fish fillets, using tweezers if necessary. Put the fillets into the refrigerator and leave them until they are very well chilled. Do not remove the fillets until needed—they must be very cold.

In a large skillet, melt the butter over low heat. Add the lemon juice, thyme, pepper, cayenne pepper and salt. Stir well and cook for 10 minutes. Pour the mixture into a large, shallow dish or bowl and cool.

Heat a large, cast-iron skillet over high heat until it is very hot. Do not grease the skillet.

Remove the fish fillets from the refrigerator and dip them into the cooled butter mixture. In batches, put the fillets into the skillet. The fish will turn black and cook almost instantly. Turn and quickly cook on the other side. There will be a lot of smoke in the kitchen. Remove the fillets from the skillet and keep warm on a plate. Cook the remaining fillets as above.

After all the fish have been cooked, add the remaining butter mixture to the skillet. Cook over high heat, stirring to loosen the brown bits on the sides and bottom of the skillet, until the butter is dark brown.

Spoon the browned butter over the fish and serve immediately.

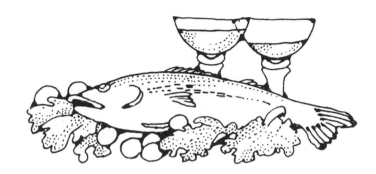

PECAN HALIBUT STEAKS

serves 4

4 8-ounce halibut steaks
1 teaspoon salt
1 teaspoon black pepper
4 tablespoons flour
5 tablespoons butter
4 tablespoons corn oil
2 tablespoons lemon juice
½ cup pecan halves
2 celery stalks, peeled and slivered
1 sweet red bell pepper, slivered

•

Wash and dry the halibut steaks. Preheat the oven to the lowest setting.

On a plate, combine 1 teaspoon of salt and 1 teaspoon of black pepper with the flour.

In a large skillet, over low heat, melt 2 tablespoons of the butter and heat the corn oil.

While the oil is heating, rub the steaks with the lemon juice. Dredge each steak in the flour, shake off the excess and put it into the skillet. Cook the steaks for 5 minutes on each side. Drain them well on paper towels. Gently pat them dry with more towels, then transfer the steaks to a serving platter. Put the platter into the oven.

To the same skillet, add the remaining butter, the pecan halves, celery, red pepper and salt to taste. Cook over medium heat for 8 minutes, stirring constantly.

Remove the platter from the oven and, using a slotted spoon, cover the halibut steaks with the pecan and vegetable mixture. Serve at once.

NEW ORLEANS POMPANO EN PAPILLOTE

serves 4

8 pompano fillets
1½ teaspoons butter
1½ teaspoons flour
½ cup white wine
salt to taste
black pepper to taste
8 large shrimp, cooked and chopped
½ cup crabmeat, cooked and flaked

•

Preheat the oven to 450°F.

Cut parchment paper or heavy aluminum foil into squares big enough to fold around 2 fish fillets. Place 2 fillets on each piece of paper or foil.

In a saucepan, melt the butter. Stir in the flour. Slowly add the white wine and cook over low heat, stirring constantly, until the mixture is smooth and thick. Season to taste with the salt and pepepr.

Spoon the sauce over the fish. Top with the chopped shrimp and crabmeat. Fold the parchment paper or foil over the fish to form a leakproof package.

Put the package on a baking sheet and bake for 15 minutes. If parchment paper is used, it will puff and brown. Serve immediately in the paper or foil package.

CRAWFISH CREOLE

serves 6

2 bay leaves
¼ teaspoon whole cloves
12 black peppercorns
1 parsley sprig
1 cinnamon stick
2 cups milk
2 tablespoons butter
2 tablespoons flour
1 teaspoon cayenne pepper
1 teaspoon hot red-pepper sauce
1 teaspoon nutmeg
salt to taste
3 tomatoes, seeded and finely chopped
36 crawfish, shelled and diced
12 mushrooms, finely chopped

•

Put the bay leaves, cloves, pepper-corns, parsley and cinnamon stick on a square of cheesecloth. Tie the square closed to make a herb bouquet. Set aside.

In a medium-sized saucepan, bring the milk to a boil over medium heat. While the milk heats, melt the butter in a large saucepan. Add the flour and cook, stirring often, for 3 minutes. When the milk boils, gradually stir it into the butter mixture. Stir in the cayenne pepper, hot red-pepper sauce, nutmeg and salt to taste. Add the herb bouquet and cook over medium heat for 15 minutes.

Remove the herb bouquet and add the tomatoes, crawfish meat and mushrooms. Cook over medium heat for 5 minutes, stirring often. Serve hot.

BARBECUED HALIBUT

serves 4

4 8-ounce halibut steaks
⅓ cup brandy
⅓ cup lemon juice
¼ teaspoon dried dill
1 bay leaf
1 medium red onion, thinly sliced
½ lemon, thinly sliced
⅓ cup chili sauce
2 tablespoons melted butter

•

Combine the brandy, lemon juice, dill and bay leaf in a shallow bowl. Add the halibut steaks to the bowl and top with the lemon and onion slices. Cover and refrigerate for 1 hour.

Remove the bowl from the refrigerator. Drain the steaks, reserving the marinade. Discard the onion and lemon slices. Place the steaks on a well-oiled grill over hot coals.

In a small bowl combine the chili sauce, butter, and reserved marinade. Baste the steaks every 2 minutes with the mixture as they cook. Grill the steaks 5 to 6 minutes on each side.

BROILED HALIBUT STEAKS WITH APRICOT SAUCE

serves 6

¾ pound fresh apricots, peeled, pitted
and halved
4 tablespoons sugar
6 8-ounce halibut steaks
2 tablespoons olive oil
2 teaspoons oregano
1 teaspoon black pepper
3 tablespoons lemon juice
1 tablespoon paprika
1 tablespoon finely chopped fresh mint

•

Put the apricots in a bowl and add 2 cups warm water. Let soak for 3 to 4 hours.

Transfer the apricots and the soaking liquid to a large skillet. Simmer over low heat for 30 minutes. Pour the apricot mixture into a bowl and stir in the sugar. Set aside.

Put the halibut steaks into a large baking dish and set aside.

In a small mixing bowl combine the olive oil, oregano, pepper, mint and lemon juice. Pour the mixture over the fish steaks. Cover the dish and marinate the steaks for 30 minutes.

Preheat the broiler.

Put the halibut steaks on a rack in the broiler pan. Reserve the marinade. Sprinkle the steaks with the paprika.

Broil the fish for 10 minutes, basting the steaks with the reserved marinade every 2 minutes. Carefully turn the steaks and cook for 6 minutes

more, continuing to baste every 2 minutes.

Transfer the steaks to a serving platter and sprinkle with the mint. Put the apricot sauce into a serving bowl. Serve the steaks immediately with the sauce on the side.

STUFFED POMPANO

serves 4

4 small whole pompanos
1 pound cooked shrimp, shelled and
deveined
1 egg, well beaten
½ teaspoon salt
¼ teaspoon black pepper
⅛ teaspoon cayenne pepper
3 tablespoons sherry
1 cup light cream

•

Preheat the oven to 350°F.

Clean and wash the fish. Split the fish, leaving the heads and tails intact.

Place the fish in a greased, shallow baking dish. The dish should be large enough to hold all the fish in one layer.

Chop the shrimp finely. In a small bowl, combine the shrimp, egg, salt, black pepper, cayenne pepper, sherry and ½ cup of the light cream.

Stuff the cavities of the fish with the shrimp mixture. Pour the remaining cream over the fish and bake for 40 minutes. Baste occasionally. Serve the fish hot with the pan juices.

BAKED REDFISH

serves 4

**1 4-pound redfish
3 to 4 tablespoons butter
salt to taste
cayenne pepper to taste
6 shrimps, cooked and coarsely
chopped
¼ cup chopped capers
lemon wedges for garnish**

•

Preheat the oven to 400°F.

Clean and wash the fish. Pat dry.

Place 2 tablespoons of butter, cut up into small pieces inside the fish. Dot the outside of the fish with the remaining butter. Season the fish to taste with salt and cayenne pepper.

Place the fish in a well-buttered shallow baking dish. Cover it with a piece of well-buttered brown paper or aluminum foil cut to fit. Bake for 40 minutes or until the fish flakes easily with a fork.

Five minutes before the fish is ready, remove it from the oven. Sprinkle the capers and shrimp around the fish. Return to the oven for 5 minutes.

Serve surrounded with the shrimp and capers and garnished with lemon wedges.

DEEP-FRIED PORGY

serves 4

**3 pounds porgy or butterfish fillets,
unskinned
2 teaspoons salt
½ teaspoon black pepper
1 cup yellow cornmeal
lard or oil for deep frying**

•

Wash and dry the fillets. Score them on the fleshy side with a sharp knife, making approximately 3 small slashes per fillet.

Season the fillets well with salt and pepper on both sides. Dip them into the cornmeal. Make sure the fillets are coated evenly. Gently shake off the excess cornmeal.

In a large deep skillet heat a ½-inch layer of oil or lard. When it is very hot, add the fish. Fry for 4 minutes on the first side. Turn the fillets carefully and fry for 3 to 4 minutes longer or until they are golden brown. Drain the fillets well on paper towels and serve hot.

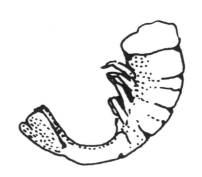

BLACKENED REDFISH

serves 8

8 8-ounce skinned redfish or any other
firm white fish fillets
2 cups sweet butter
¼ cup lemon juice
1 tablespoon dried thyme
2 teaspoons black pepper
1½ teaspoons cayenne pepper
1 teaspoon salt

•

Remove any small bones from the fish fillets, using tweezers if necessary. Put the fillets into the refrigerator and leave them until they are very well chilled. Do not remove the fillets until needed—they must be very cold.

In a large skillet, melt the butter over low heat. Add the lemon juice, thyme, pepper, cayenne pepper and salt. Stir well and cook for 10 minutes. Pour the mixture into a large, shallow dish or bowl and cool.

Heat a large, cast-iron skillet over high heat, until it is very hot. Do not grease the skillet.

Remove the fish fillets from the refrigerator and dip them into the cooled butter mixture. In batches, put the fillets into the skillet. The fish will turn black and cook almost instantly. Turn and quickly cook on the other side. There will be a lot of smoke in the kitchen. Remove the fillets from the skillet and keep warm on a plate. Cook the remaining fillets as above.

After all the fish have been cooked, add the remaining butter mixture to the skillet. Cook over high heat, stirring to loosen the brown bits on the sides and bottom of the skillet, until the butter is dark brown.

Spoon the browned butter over the fish and serve immediately.

SMOKED REDFISH

serves 4

1 4-pound redfish
2 garlic cloves, crushed
salt to taste
black pepper to taste
1 tablespoon grated lemon rind
½ cup lemon juice
¼ pound melted butter
2 tablespoons Worcestershire sauce
½ teaspoon hot red-pepper sauce
1 teaspoon chopped parsley

•

Clean and wash the fish. Pat it dry. Rub the fish with the garlic, black pepper and lemon rind.

In a small bowl combine the lemon juice, butter, Worcestershire sauce, hot red-pepper sauce and parsley. Mix well.

Cover the head and tail of the fish with pieces of aluminum foil.

Place the fish on an oiled grill over low coals. Cover the grill and smoke the fish for about 1 hour or until the fish flakes easily. Do not overcook. Baste the fish with the lemon sauce every 15 minutes.

Cool before serving.

Red Rice

Tomato Soup with Beef and Okra

Barbecued Halibut

BAKED RED SNAPPER

serves 6

1 4-pound red snapper, cleaned
4 tablespoons butter
1 teaspoon cayenne pepper
6 shrimp, cooked and chopped
4 tablespoons capers, chopped
1 tablespoon lemon juice
1 tablespoon chopped parsley
salt to taste
2 lemons, cut into wedges

•

Wash and dry the red snapper. Preheat the oven to 400°F. Lightly butter a shallow baking dish large enough to hold the fish.

In a medium-sized mixing bowl, combine 2 tablespoons of the butter, cut in small pieces, with the cayenne pepper, shrimp, capers, lemon juice, parsley and salt to taste. Mix carefully but thoroughly. Stuff the fish with the mixture. Close the cavity with wooden toothpicks. Rub the outside of the fish with the remaining butter.

Put the fish into the baking dish and cover with aluminum foil. Bake for 45 minutes.

Carefully transfer the fish to a platter, remove the toothpicks, garnish with the lemon wedges and serve.

GULF-STYLE RED SNAPPER

serves 4

4 8-ounce red snapper fillets
salt to taste
black pepper to taste
1 teaspoon oregano
2 tablespoons butter, softened
4 carrots, chopped
1 celery stalk, chopped
2 tablespoons chopped parsley
6 uncooked shrimp, peeled, deveined
1 cup dry vermouth
1 bay leaf

•

Wash and dry the red snapper fillets. Rub them with the salt, pepper and oregano. Put the fillets into a buttered casserole dish. Preheat the oven to 400°F.

In a large mixing bowl, combine the butter, carrots, celery, parsley, shrimp, dry vermouth and bay leaf, mix thoroughly. Pour the sauce over the fish.

Cover the dish and bake the fish for 30 minutes, or until the fish flakes with the touch of a fork. Serve hot from the casserole dish.

LEMON-LIME RED SNAPPER

serves 4

4 chopped scallions
¼ cup lime juice
2 teaspoons grated lemon rind
salt to taste
¼ teaspoon nutmeg
¼ teaspoon cinnamon
4 8-ounce red snapper fillets, with skin

•

In a mixing bowl combine the scallions, lime juice, grated lemon rind and salt to taste. Pour the mixture into a shallow baking dish large enough to hold all the fillets in one layer.

Rinse and dry the fillets. Put the fillets skin-side down into the baking dish, then turn them over. Allow the fish to stand in the marinade, skin-side up, for 30 minutes at room temperature.

Preheat the oven to 400°F.

Turn the fillets skin-side down and sprinkle them with the nutmeg and cinnamon. Cover the dish and bake for 15 minutes, or until the fish flakes easily with a fork. Baste every 5 minutes with the pan juices. Serve hot from the baking dish.

RED HOT SNAPPER

serves 4

4 8-ounce red snapper fillets
2 tablespoons olive oil
1 garlic clove, finely chopped
1 large onion, chopped
½ cup of pimento-stuffed green olives, sliced
½ small red bell pepper, chopped
1 teaspoon ground cumin
1 teaspoon chili powder
1 dried hot red chili pepper, finely chopped
6 tablespoons lemon juice
6 tablespoons orange juice
salt to taste
black pepper to taste

•

Wash and dry the red snapper fillets. Put them into a lightly buttered baking dish. Preheat the oven to 375°F.

In a large skillet over medium-low heat, heat the olive oil. Add the garlic and chopped onion. Cook, stirring constantly, until the onion is soft. Add the sliced olives, sweet red bell pepper, cumin, chili powder and chili pepper and mix well. Add the lemon juice, orange juice and salt and pepper to taste and stir until well blended. Simmer for 5 minutes.

Pour the sauce over the fish. Bake, uncovered, for 20 minutes. Carefully transfer the fillets to a serving platter. Pour the sauce over them and serve.

ROASTED RED SNAPPER WITH FRESH MINT

serves 4

1 3-pound red snapper, cleaned
salt to taste
black pepper to taste
15 fresh mint sprigs
3 tablespoons olive oil
1 teaspoon paprika
½ cup clarified butter
3 tablespoons lemon juice

•

Preheat the oven to 400°F.

Season the cavity of the fish with salt and pepper. Stuff the cavity with 7 mint sprigs, then close it with wooden toothpicks. Rub the outside of the fish with the olive oil, salt and pepper. Put the fish on a rack in a baking pan and sprinkle it with the paprika. Bake for 45 minutes.

While the fish bakes, chop the remaining mint sprigs. Put the clarified butter in a small saucepan over low heat. Add the chopped mint and lemon juice and mix well. Simmer for 2 minutes. Strain the sauce through a cheesecloth, discarding the bits of mint that remain in the cloth.

Carefully transfer the fish to a serving platter. Remove the toothpicks. Pour the minted butter sauce over the fish and serve.

SMOKED RED SNAPPER

serves 6

4 pounds red snapper fillets
2 garlic cloves, finely chopped
grated rind of 1 lemon
salt to taste
black pepper to taste
¾ cup lemon juice
8 tablespoons butter
2 tablespoons Worcestershire sauce
½ teaspoon hot red-pepper sauce
1 tablespoon finely chopped parsley
1 teaspoon liquid smoke

•

Wash and dry the red snapper fillets. In a small bowl, combine the garlic, grated lemon rind and salt and pepper to taste. Rub the fillets with the mixture.

In a large skillet, melt the butter over low heat. Stir in the lemon juice, Worcestershire sauce, hot red-pepper sauce, liquid smoke and chopped parsley. Mix well.

Put the fillets into the skillet and cook over low heat for 1 hour, basting the fish with the sauce every 15 minutes. Use a loose-fitting cover over the skillet.

Cool to room temperature before serving.

BACON-BAKED ROCKFISH

serves 4

1 3-pound rockfish
salt to taste
black pepper to taste
flour
6 thick bacon strips
1 large onion, diced
½ cup chopped scallion
3 tablespoons brandy
1 cup water

●

Preheat the oven to 350°F.

Make three ½-inch-deep cuts in each side of the fish. Sprinkle the fish with salt, pepper and flour on both sides. Wrap the bacon strips around the fish.

Put the fish in a shallow baking dish. Sprinkle the onions and scallions on top of the fish. Pour the water and brandy into the baking dish and cover. Bake for 20 minutes, then remove the cover and continue to bake until the fish is well-browned. Serve with Worcestershire sauce.

FRIED SCALLOPS

serves 4

2 pounds bay scallops
4 tablespoons flour
4 tablespoons unflavored breadcrumbs
½ teaspoon cayenne pepper
4 tablespoons grated Romano cheese
1 tablespoon finely chopped parsley
1 egg
¼ cup milk
1 cup olive oil

●

Wash the scallops and put them on a clean kitchen towel to dry.

In a large, shallow bowl combine the flour, breadcrumbs, cayenne pepper, Romano cheese and parsley. In another bowl, beat the egg and the milk together. Heat the olive oil in a large skillet to 375°F.

Dip the scallops into the egg mixture and then roll them in the flour mixture. Cook the scallops in the skillet for 4 minutes, using tongs to turn them. Transfer the scallops to paper towels to drain. Serve immediately.

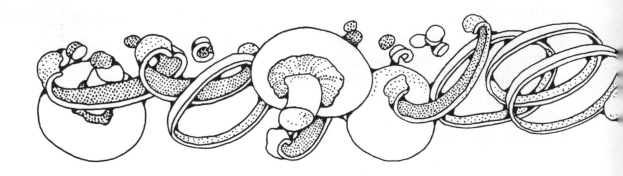

SCALLOPS IN BUTTER AND BRANDY SAUCE

serves 4

2 pounds sea scallops
1 teaspoon salt
1 cup butter
4 tablespoons brandy
1 tablespoon chopped parsley

•

Wash the scallops and put them into a saucepan with the salt and enough water to cover. Bring the water to a simmer and gently cook the scallops for 3 minutes. Drain well in a colander.

While the scallops are draining, melt the butter in a large skillet over medium-high heat. Add the scallops. Cook, stirring gently, until the butter turns light brown.

In a small saucepan, heat the brandy until it sizzles. Carefully ignite the brandy and pour it over the scallops. When the flame dies out, transfer the scallops to a serving bowl, sprinkle with parsley and serve.

SCALLOP STEW

serves 4

2 pounds sea scallops
½ cup dry vermouth
2 garlic cloves, finely chopped
6 tablespoons olive oil
1 large red onion, thinly sliced and broken into rings
6 plum tomatoes, peeled and chopped
4 tablespoons butter
salt to taste
black pepper to taste
2 tablespoons chopped parsley

•

Wash the scallops, but do not dry them. Put them into a small bowl, add the vermouth and garlic, mix well and let stand for 30 minutes.

In a large skillet, heat the olive oil. Add the onion rings and cook, stirring constantly, until they turn golden. Add the tomatoes, cover the skillet and cook until the tomatoes are soft. Add the butter, the scallops and the marinade and salt and pepper to taste. Simmer for 5 minutes, uncovered. Stir in the parsley. Transfer to a serving bowl and serve.

BROILED MARINATED SHRIMP

serves 6

2 garlic cloves, crushed
2 tablespoons red wine vinegar
½ cup olive oil
2 teaspoons ground cumin
2 teaspoons chili powder
½ teaspoon black pepper
3 teaspoons dried basil
2 pounds medium shrimp, shelled and deveined

•

In a small bowl combine the garlic and vinegar. Set aside.

In a large mixing bowl, combine the olive oil, cumin, chili powder, black pepper and basil. Add the shrimp and mix well. Add the garlic and vinegar mixture and mix well again. Cover the bowl and refrigerate for 3 hours.

Preheat the broiler. Remove the shrimp from the marinade and put them in a broiler pan. Brush the shrimp with the marinade. Broil for 7 minutes, brushing the shrimp with the marinade every 2 minutes.

Transfer the shrimp to a serving platter. Pour the remaining marinade over them and serve.

BROILED SHRIMP IN GARLIC SAUCE

serves 6

2½ pounds large shrimp
4 garlic cloves, finely chopped
½ onion, finely chopped
4 tablespoons chopped parsley
8 tablespoons butter
1 teaspoon oregano
salt to taste
black pepper to taste
1 teaspoon paprika

•

Shell the shrimp, but leave the tails on. Remove the veins. With a sharp knife, butterfly the shrimp down the back. Wash the shrimp thoroughly. Flatten them on paper towels and pat dry with more paper towels. Set aside. Preheat the broiler.

In a saucepan, combine the garlic, onion, parsley and butter. Cook over low heat, stirring constantly. As the butter melts add the oregano and salt and pepper to taste.

Keep the butter mixture over very low heat. Dip each shrimp into the mixture then put it on a large shallow broiler pan. The shrimp should fit in a single layer. Sprinkle the shrimp with the paprika. Broil for 7 minutes, or until the shrimp are sizzling.

Transfer the shrimp to a serving platter. Pour the remaining butter sauce over them and serve.

FRIED SHRIMP ROMANO

serves 4

4 tablespoons olive oil
salt to taste
2 tablespoons lemon juice
2 pounds large shrimp
½ cup flour
4 tablespoons cracker meal
4 tablespoons grated Romano cheese
black pepper to taste
1 egg
½ cup warm water
1 cup vegetable oil

•

In a large mixing bowl, combine 3 tablespoons of the olive oil, salt and lemon juice. Set aside.

Shell the shrimp and remove the veins. Add the shrimp to the marinade in the mixing bowl. Mix well. Set aside for 30 minutes.

While the shrimp are marinating, in a small bowl combine the flour, cracker meal and the grated cheese.

In another bowl, combine salt, pepper, 1 tablespoon of olive oil, the egg and the warm water. Beat until well mixed.

In a large skillet, heat the vegetable oil to 375°F. While the oil is heating, gradually add the flour mixture to the egg mixture, beating constantly until smooth.

Remove the shrimp from the marinade with a slotted spoon. Skewer each shrimp on a wooden toothpick. Dip each shrimp into the batter,

then put it into the hot oil. Cook until the shrimp are golden brown. Drain them on paper towels, transfer them to a serving platter and serve.

LOUISIANA SHRIMP

serves 6

2 pounds shrimp
4 tablespoons butter
1 cup unflavored breadcrumbs
2 garlic cloves, finely chopped
½ teaspoon hot red-pepper sauce
salt to taste
¾ cup dry vermouth
¼ teaspoon black pepper
¼ teaspoon cayenne pepper

•

In a large pot, bring 3 quarts of water to boil over high heat. Add the shrimp. When the water returns to a boil, reduce the heat and simmer the shrimp for 5 minutes.

Drain the shrimp, shell them and remove the veins. Put the shrimp on paper towels to dry.

Preheat the oven to 350°F. Grease a 15-inch baking dish with butter.

In a medium-sized saucepan, melt the butter over low heat. Remove the pan from the heat and mix in the breadcrumbs, garlic, hot red-pepper sauce and salt to taste. Mix well and return the pan to extremely low heat.

Quickly arrange the shrimp in the baking pan. Pour the vermouth and then the butter mixture over them. Sprinkle with black pepper and cayenne. Bake for 20 minutes. Serve hot.

SHRIMP WITH ZUCCHINI

serves 4

1 pound medium shrimp, shelled and
deveined
3 tablespoons olive oil
1 tablespoon lemon juice
1 small green bell pepper, diced
1 small red bell pepper, diced
2 garlic cloves, finely chopped
1 large onion, coarsely chopped
2 large tomatoes, seeded and coarsely
chopped
2 small zucchini, thinly sliced
salt to taste
black pepper to taste

•

Heat the olive oil in a large skillet. Add the lemon juice and mix well. Add the green bell pepper and red bell pepper and cook, stirring constantly, over medium heat for 3 minutes. Add the garlic and onion and cook, stirring constantly, for 3 minutes longer. Add the zucchini and tomatoes and salt and pepper to taste. Stir well, cover the skillet and simmer for 5 minutes.

Add the shrimp to the vegetables in the skillet and stir well. Cover the skillet and simmer for 5 minutes longer. Transfer the mixture to a serving bowl and serve at once.

SHRIMP ON TAP

serves 4

3 cups beer
2 garlic cloves, chopped
1 teaspoon celery seeds
2 tablespoons finely chopped parsley
1 teaspoon hot red-pepper sauce
3 tablespoons lemon juice
salt to taste
2 pounds medium shrimp, shelled and
deveined
8 tablespoons butter

•

In a large saucepan combine the beer, garlic, celery seed, parsley, hot red-pepper sauce, lemon juice and salt to taste. Over medium-high heat bring the beer to a boil.

When the beer is at full boil, add the shrimp. When it returns to the boil, reduce the heat and simmer the shrimp for 5 minutes.

In a small saucepan, melt the butter over low heat. Set aside in a warm place.

Drain the shrimp and transfer them to a serving bowl. Pour the melted butter into four small bowls for dipping. Serve immediately.

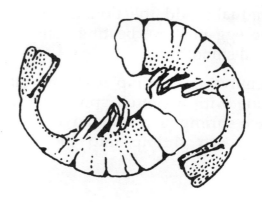

SHRIMP WITH BLACKEYED PEAS

serves 6

¾ cup vegetable oil
½ cup finely chopped onion
2 garlic cloves, chopped
½ pound shrimp, shelled, deveined
and cut into thirds
1 cup diced ham
½ cup tomato sauce
1 small hot red pepper, seeded and
finely chopped
2 cups cooked blackeyed peas

•

Heat the oil in a large saucepan. Add the onion and garlic and sauté until the onion is transparent, about 4 minutes. Add the shrimp and cook for 8 minutes. Add the ham and tomato sauce, reduce the heat and simmer for 10 minutes. Add the hot red pepper, reduce the heat to very low and simmer for 5 minutes longer. Add the blackeyed peas and cook until the peas are heated through, about 5 minutes.

SHRIMP CREOLE

serves 8

2 cups water
3 garlic cloves, finely chopped
4 whole cloves
1 teaspoon cinnamon
3 cups canned whole tomatoes
2 tablespoons chopped parsley
4 bay leaves
1 teaspoon oregano
2 teaspoons hot red pepper flakes
1 teaspoon black pepper
½ teaspoon cayenne pepper
½ teaspoon hot red-pepper sauce
2 teaspoons salt
1 red bell pepper, coarsely chopped
1 large head celery, with leaves,
coarsely chopped
3 pounds medium-sized shrimp,
shelled and deveined

•

In a large pot combine the water, garlic, cloves, cinnamon, tomatoes, parsley, bay leaves, oregano, red pepper flakes, black pepper, cayenne pepper, hot red-pepper sauce and salt. Bring the mixture to a boil over high heat.

Add the red bell pepper and celery. When the liquid returns to the boil, reduce the heat to medium and simmer for 20 minutes.

Add the shrimp to the pot and raise the heat. Simmer for 10 minutes. Remove the pot from the heat and let cool for 20 to 30 minutes. Serve at room temperature.

SHRIMP AND CORN SOUFFLÉ

serves 6

6 ears corn
2 pounds small shrimp
3 eggs, separated
2 teaspoons sugar
1 tablespoon cream
1 tablespoon butter, melted

●

In a large pot, bring 3 quarts of water to a boil over high heat. Add the shrimp. When the water returns to a boil, reduce the heat and simmer the shrimp for 5 minutes. Drain the shrimp, remove the shells and veins. Wash the shrimp and dry them. Put them into a large bowl.

Preheat the oven to 300°F. Grease a 2-quart soufflé dish.

Shuck the corn and remove the silk. Cut the kernels off the cob, and mix the corn kernels with the shrimp.

In a large mixing bowl, beat the egg yolks. Stir in the sugar, cream and melted butter. Add the corn and shrimp. Mix well.

In another bowl, beat the egg whites until they are stiff. Fold the egg whites into the shrimp mixture.

Spoon the mixture into the prepared soufflé dish. Cover the dish with the aluminum foil and set it in a pan of hot water. (The water should come about three-quarters up the side of the soufflé dish.) Bake for 45 minutes.

Remove the foil from the dish and bake for 15 minutes more, or until the top is golden brown. Serve immediately.

STUFFED SOLE IN CREOLE SAUCE

serves 6

7 tablespoons butter
4 tablespoons finely chopped onion
4 tablespoons finely chopped celery
2 tablespoons finely chopped red bell pepper
2 tablespoons flour
½ cup light cream
½ cup fine unflavored breadcrumbs
½ teaspoon oregano
1 cup cooked crabmeat, flaked
1 cup cooked shrimp, chopped
4 tablespoons chopped parsley
2 teaspoons Worcestershire sauce
1 teaspoon hot red-pepper sauce
salt to taste
black pepper to taste
6 8-ounce sole fillets

CREOLE SAUCE:

2 tablespoons butter
4 cups canned tomatoes
2 garlic cloves, finely chopped
1 bay leaf
¼ teaspoon cayenne pepper
salt to taste
black pepper to taste
1 tablespoon flour

●

Preheat the oven to 350°F. In a large skillet melt 4 tablespoons of butter. Add to the butter the onion, celery and red bell pepper. Cook over low heat, stirring frequently, until the vegetables are tender, about 5 minutes. Carefully stir in the flour and continue stirring until smooth. Add the cream and continue over low heat, stirring constantly, until the mixture has thickened. Remove the skillet from the heat and add the breadcrumbs, oregano, crabmeat, shrimp, parsley, Worcestershire sauce, Tabasco sauce and salt and pepper to taste. Mix well.

Lay the sole fillets out on a working surface. Spoon one-sixth of the mixture on each fillet. Roll up the fillet and secure with a wooden toothpick. Melt the remaining butter in a small saucepan. Brush the stuffed sole fillets with the melted butter. Put them into a baking dish and bake them for 20 minutes.

While the fish is cooking, prepare the Creole sauce. In a medium-sized saucepan melt 1 tablespoon butter. Add the tomatoes, garlic, bay leaf, cayenne pepper and salt and pepper to taste. Cook over medium heat for 20 minutes.

In a small saucepan, melt the remaining butter; stir in the flour. Continue to cook over low heat, stirring constantly, until the flour turns light brown. Add the flour and butter mixture to the tomato mixture and stir until blended.

Reduce the oven temperature to 300°F. Remove the stuffed sole fillets from the oven. Pour the Creole sauce over the fillets. Bake for 30 minutes more. Serve hot.

TROUT WITH ALMONDS AND PINE NUTS

serves 4

4 8-ounce trout
6 tablespoons butter
3 tablespoons olive oil
1 teaspoon oregano
½ teaspoon salt
1 teaspoon black pepper
1 teaspoon paprika
3 tablespoons lemon juice
2 tablespoons dry sherry
2 tablespoons finely chopped parsley
4 tablespoons sliced almonds
4 tablespoons pine nuts

Clean the trout and rub them with the olive oil. Combine the oregano, salt, pepper and paprika. Put the fish on a platter and rub the inside and outside of each one with the oregano mixture. Set aside.

In a large skillet melt 4 tablespoons of the butter. Add the lemon juice, sherry and parsley and mix well. Add the almonds and pine nuts and cook over low heat until they start to turn golden.

With a large spoon, push the nuts to one side of the skillet. Add the remaining butter. When it has melted, put the fish into the skillet, covering each one with some of the nuts. Partly cover the skillet and cook the fish over low heat for 15 minutes on each side, or until they flake with the touch of a fork. Transfer the fish to a serving platter and serve.

SOUTHERN-STYLE TARTAR SAUCE

makes 1½ cups

2 tablespoons tarragon vinegar
⅛ teaspoon cayenne pepper
¼ cup finely chopped dill pickle
6 shallots, finely chopped
1 tablespoon chopped chives
1 tablespoon chopped parsley
1 teaspoon capers, finely chopped
1 cup mayonnaise
1 teaspoon dry mustard

•

In a bowl combine the vinegar and cayenne pepper. Whisk until the cayenne dissolves. Add the pickles, shallots, chives, parsley and capers. Stir well. Beat in the mayonnaise and mustard.

Cover and refrigerate for 3 hours before serving. This sauce will keep for up to 2 days in the refrigerator.

Poultry and Eggs

BACON-WRAPPED CHICKEN WITH ASPARAGUS

serves 6

6 whole boneless and skinless chicken breasts
12 asparagus spears
12 tablespoons white sauce
1 tablespoon chopped parsley
1 teaspoon cayenne pepper
1 teaspoon paprika
12 strips bacon
wooden toothpicks

•

Preheat the oven to 375°F. Open the breasts and place 2 asparagus spears into each. Top the asparagus with 2 tablespoons of white sauce and sprinkle with the parsley, cayenne pepper and paprika.

Close the breasts and wrap with 2 strips of bacon each. Secure the breasts with toothpicks and place in a shallow pan.

Bake for 30 minutes and carefully turn over. Bake for 15 minutes more and serve.

CHICKEN BREASTS WITH APRICOT SAUCE

serves 6

¾ pound fresh apricots, pitted and coarsely chopped
2 cups water
5 tablespoons sugar
¼ cup butter
6 boneless and skinless chicken breasts
3 tablespoons chopped parsley
2 teaspoons paprika

•

Combine the apricots, water and sugar in a saucepan and bring to a boil. Simmer over low heat for 1 hour.

Melt the butter in a skillet and lightly brown the chicken on one side. Sprinkle with half the parsley and paprika, turn and lightly brown the other side.

Sprinkle with the remaining parsley and paprika. Turn and simmer over low heat until cooked, about 30 minutes.

Transfer the breasts to a platter and pour the sauce over them before serving.

BARBECUED CHICKEN

serves 10

30 chicken pieces
½ cup melted butter
6 tablespoons lemon juice
¼ cup chili sauce
1 tablespoon Worcestershire sauce
1 teaspoon salt
1 teaspoon dried red pepper flakes
½ cup white wine

•

Rinse the pieces of chicken and pat dry. Start the coals in the barbecue.

Combine the butter, lemon juice, chili sauce, Worcestershire sauce, salt, red pepper flakes and wine in a deep saucepan and place on the grill in a warm spot.

Dip each piece of chicken into the sauce, and allow excess to run off back into the saucepan. Grill until done, about 25 minutes, turning and basting often.

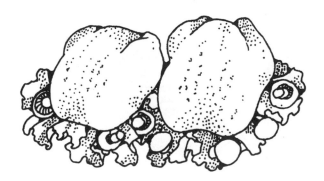

CHICKABOBS

serves 6

3 whole boneless and skinless chicken
breasts, cut into 30 pieces
24 chunks pineapple
24 chunks red bell pepper
24 chunks green bell pepper
18 small white onions
6 12-inch skewers
¼ pound butter, melted
4 tablespoons dry sherry
3 tablespoons lemon juice
1 tablespoon oregano
1 teaspoon salt
1 teaspoon cayenne pepper

•

Heat the coals in the barbecue. Spear onto each of the skewers in the following order, one chunk at a time, chicken; onion; green pepper; red pepper; pineapple; chicken; pineapple; red pepper; green pepper; chicken; onion; green pepper; red pepper; pineapple; chicken; pineapple; red pepper; green pepper; onion; chicken.

Combine the remaining ingredients in a small saucepan and place on warm part of grill. Place the skewers on the grill and generously brush them with the sauce. Turn and brush the other side. Grill until cooked, brushing often, about 25 minutes.

CHICKEN CORDON BLEU

serves 6

6 boneless, skinless chicken breasts
1 lemon
1 tablespoon chopped parsley
1 teaspoon salt
1 teaspoon cayenne pepper
¼ cup olive oil
6 thick slices Swiss cheese
6 ham slices
12 tablespoons white sauce
1 teaspoon paprika

•

Squeeze the lemon over the chicken and let stand for 10 minutes. Rub the parsley, salt, and cayenne pepper into the chicken.

Heat the oil in a skillet. Preheat the oven to 300°F. Brown the chicken in the oil and drain on paper towels. Place the chicken on a broiler pan with a rack and cover first with the cheese and then the ham. Spoon 2 tablespoons of white sauce over each. Sprinkle with paprika. Place in the oven and bake for 10 minutes.

CHICKEN FRICASSEE

serves 6

4 pounds chicken pieces
4 cups water
3 carrots, cut in half
4 celery stalks, cut in thirds
1 large onion, cut into wedges
1 bay leaf
¼ teaspoon rosemary
2 teaspoons salt
½ teaspoon black pepper
2 cups elbow macaroni

•

Wash the chicken pieces and pat dry. Season with salt and pepper. Bring the water to a boil and add the carrots, celery, onion, bay leaf, rosemary, and bring back to a boil. Reduce the heat and simmer for 10 minutes.

Add the chicken pieces and continue to simmer for 1 hour. Stir in the macaroni, adding water if there is not enough to cover the macaroni. Bring back to a boil and reduce the heat. Simmer until the macaroni is tender, about 15 to 20 minutes.

CHICKEN CURRY

serves 10

4 pounds boneless and skinless
chicken meat, cut into chunks
4 cups water
1 cup white wine
1 lemon, sliced
3 onions
8 celery stalks
3 green apples, cored and diced
½ cup vegetable oil
2 tablespoons curry powder
½ teaspoon black pepper
½ teaspoon ground ginger
2 teaspoons hot red-pepper sauce
1 tablespoon Worcestershire sauce
⅓ cup flour
½ cup water
1 cup grated unsweetened coconut
3 egg yolks, beaten
1 cup evaporated milk
¼ pound seedless raisins
¼ pound unsalted cashews, halved

•

Combine the chicken, water, wine, lemon, 1 onion and 2 celery stalks in a large pot and bring to a boil. Reduce the heat and simmer for 20 minutes. Chop remaining onion and celery.

Drain the chicken and reserve the liquid. Discard lemon, onion and celery stalks. Chop the chicken meat and reserve.

Sauté the chopped onion, celery and apples in the oil until tender. Stir in the curry powder and simmer for 3 minutes. Stir in the pepper, ginger, hot red-pepper sauce, Worcestershire sauce and reserved cooking liquid and bring to a boil.

Stir in a mixture of the flour and water and lower the heat. Simmer for 20 minutes, stirring constantly.

Stir in the coconut meat and continue to simmer for 10 minutes. Cool slightly and refrigerate overnight.

Stir in the egg yolks, evaporated milk, raisins and cashews and heat slowly until bubbling. Serve over rice.

CHICKEN POT

serves 6

4 pounds chicken pieces
½ teaspoon salt
2 lemon slices
8 small potatoes, unpeeled
4 carrots, julienned
4 celery stalks, sliced
2 onions, cut into wedges
½ pound string beans, trimmed and halved
½ cup chopped parsley
¼ teaspoon thyme
1 teaspoon salt
1 teaspoon black pepper

•

Place the chicken in a large pot and cover with water. Add the salt and bring to a boil. Reduce the heat, add the lemon slices and simmer for 30 minutes.

Add the potatoes, celery, onions, beans, parsley, thyme, salt and pepper and continue to simmer for 30 minutes more. Serve in soup bowls with lots of the broth.

CHICKEN IN PEANUT SAUCE

serves 8

3½-pound chicken, skinned, boned
and chunked
1½ cups chicken broth
1 cup water
1 teaspoon salt
1 teaspoon oregano
6 tomatoes, quartered
6 ounces tomato paste
2 large onions, cut into wedges
1 cup smooth peanut butter
1 teaspoon cayenne pepper

•

Combine the chicken broth, water, salt and oregano in a pot and bring to a boil. Lower the heat and simmer for 15 minutes.

Stir in the tomatoes, tomato paste, onions, peanut butter and cayenne pepper. Stir until smooth. Simmer for 20 minutes, stirring often. Serve over rice.

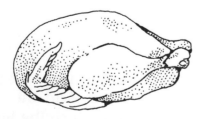

CHICKEN 'N' DUMPLINS

serves 6

3 tablespoons butter
3 pounds boneless, skinless chicken,
chunked
3 onions, cut into wedges
4 carrots, cut in 1-inch pieces
and halved
1 tablespoon chopped parsley
2 cups chicken broth
1 cup water
1 bay leaf
2 teaspoons salt
1 teaspoon black pepper
1 teaspoon oregano
3 tablespoons cornstarch
1 cup prepared biscuit mix
⅓ cup light cream
½ teaspoon poultry seasoning

•

Melt the butter in a skillet and brown the chicken. Stir in the onions, carrots, parsley, broth, water, bay leaf, salt, pepper and oregano and bring to a boil. Stir in the cornstarch and lower the heat. Simmer for 45 minutes.

Mix the biscuit mix, cream and poultry seasoning in a bowl and blend thoroughly. Drop spoonfuls of the batter into the skillet and simmer until the dumplings are cooked, about 20 to 25 minutes.

CHICKEN WITH PINE NUTS

serves 4

¼ cup olive oil
4 boneless, skinless chicken breasts
¼ cup lemon juice
1 tablespoon chopped parsley
1 teaspoon salt
½ teaspoon black pepper
½ teaspoon cayenne pepper
1 red bell pepper, coarsely chopped
1 green bell pepper, coarsely chopped
1 onion, coarsely chopped
1 cup pine nuts
3 tablespoons sweet butter
¼ cup white wine

•

Heat half of the oil in a skillet and brown the chicken thoroughly. Use two forks to shred the chicken in the skillet.

Transfer the chicken to a mixing bowl and mix well with the remaining olive oil, lemon juice, parsley, salt, pepper, cayenne pepper, red and green bell peppers and onion. Cover and refrigerate for 2 hours.

Lightly brown the pine nuts in the butter in a large skillet. Stir in the chicken mixture and the wine and bring to a boil. Reduce the heat and simmer for 45 minutes. Serve over rice.

CHICKEN AND VEGETABLES IN WINE SAUCE

serves 8

4 carrots, julienned
5 stalks celery, julienned
1 pound boneless and skinless chicken thigh
1 pound boneless and skinless chicken breasts
1 red bell pepper, sliced into rings
1 green bell pepper, sliced into rings
2 large onions, sliced into wedges
½ cup white wine
¼ cup soy sauce
¼ cup lemon juice
1 tablespoon oregano
1 tablespoon chopped parsley
1 teaspoon salt
1 teaspoon black pepper
1 teaspoon paprika

•

Preheat the oven to 325°F. Combine the carrots and celery in a large roasting pan. Arrange the chicken pieces on top of the carrots and celery. Put the red and green bell pepper rings over the chicken and place the onions among the rings.

Combine the wine, soy sauce, lemon juice, oregano, parsley, salt, pepper and paprika in a blender and blend on low for 1 minute.

Pour the sauce over the chicken and bake for 1 hour and 15 minutes, tightly covered.

COQ AU VIN

serves 6

¼ pound bacon, cut into quarters
3 pounds boneless and skinless
chicken meat, chunked
meat, chunked
1 tablespoon flour
1½ cups red wine
¼ cup brandy
1 tablespoon tomato paste
2 bay leaves
1 teaspoon oregano
1 teaspoon salt
½ teaspoon black pepper
2 garlic cloves, minced
16 pearl onions
16 small white mushrooms

•

Fry the bacon in a skillet and drain on paper towels. Lightly brown the chicken chunks in the bacon drippings. Remove the chicken and drain on paper towels. Stir in the flour and sauté for 2 minutes.

Stir in the wine, brandy, tomato paste, bay leaves, oregano, salt, pepper, garlic, onions and mushrooms. Bring the mixture to a boil, reduce the heat and simmer for 20 minutes. Remove the bay leaves and stir in the chicken pieces. Continue to simmer for 10 minutes. Stir in the bacon and serve.

CORNMEAL FRIED CHICKEN

serves 4

1 4-pound chicken, cut into pieces
¾ cup cracker meal
¾ cup yellow cornmeal
1½ teaspoons cinnamon
1½ tablespoons chopped parsley
1 teaspoon salt
1 teaspoon paprika
vegetable oil or lard for frying

•

Rinse the pieces of chicken and pat dry.

Combine the cracker meal, cornmeal, cinnamon, parsley, salt and paprika in a large plastic bag and shake well.

Fill a deep, heavy skillet with oil to a depth of 2 inches. Heat the oil over moderate heat until a drop of water sizzles when dropped into it. Place a few pieces of chicken into the bag and shake until well coated. Fry until golden brown on all sides, about 20 minutes, and drain on paper towels. Repeat with the remaining chicken.

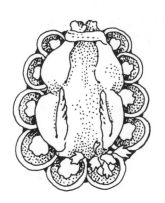

FRENCH-STYLE CHICKEN

serves 6

1 5-pound roasting chicken, with
giblets
1 onion, chopped
3 celery stalks, finely chopped
4 cups chicken broth
2 cups water
1 bay leaf
2 onions, cut into wedges
4 carrots, julienned
5 celery stalks, chopped
2 zucchini, sliced
1 tablespoon chopped parsley
½ cup brandy
½ teaspoon paprika
½ teaspoon cayenne pepper

•

Preheat the oven to 325°F. Chop the giblets and mix with the onion and 3 stalks finely chopped celery. Stuff the chicken with this mixture and skewer closed.

Place the chicken in a large roasting pan and add the chicken broth and water. Add the bay leaf and bake, covered, for 1 hour.

Add the onions, carrots, remaining celery and zucchini. Pour the brandy over the chicken. Sprinkle with the paprika and cayenne pepper and bake, uncovered, for 1 hour.

FRIED CHICKEN

serves 4

1 4-pound frying chicken cut into
pieces
1½ cups flour
1½ teaspoons paprika
1½ teaspoons dry mustard
1 teaspoon nutmeg
1 teaspoon garlic powder
vegetable oil or lard for frying
salt to taste
black pepper to taste

•

Rinse the chicken pieces and pat dry. In a large plastic bag combine the flour, paprika, mustard, nutmeg, and garlic powder. Close bag and shake well.

Fill a deep heavy skillet with oil to a depth of 2 inches. Heat the oil over moderate heat until a drop of water sizzles when dropped into it.

Sprinkle the chicken pieces with salt and pepper and place, a few pieces at a time, into the plastic bag. Shake until the pieces are well coated and put them into the hot oil. Fry until golden brown on all sides, about 20 minutes, and drain on paper towels. Repeat with the remaining chicken.

FRIED CHICKEN CUTLETS

serves 6

**6 whole chicken breasts, skinned and boned
½ cup cracker meal
½ cup flour
½ cup grated Parmesan cheese
1½ tablespoons chopped parsley
1½ teaspoons garlic powder
1 teaspoon cayenne pepper
1½ teaspoons salt
2 eggs, beaten
vegetable oil for frying**

●

Rinse the cutlets then pat dry.

Combine the cracker meal, flour, cheese, parsley, garlic powder, cayenne pepper and salt in a large plastic bag and shake well. Pour the mixture onto a large platter.
Dip the cutlets into the egg and then coat thoroughly in the cracker meal mixture.

Fill a deep, heavy skillet with oil to a depth of one-half inch. Heat the oil over moderate heat until a drop of water sizzles when dropped into it.

Fry the chicken breasts, two at a time, until golden brown on the bottom, about 10 minutes. Turn and fry on the other side. Drain on paper towels and serve with lemon wedges or on bread as sandwiches.

FRIED CHICKEN CREAM GRAVY

makes 1½ cups

**6 tablespoons drippings from frying of chicken
6 tablespoons flour
1 teaspoon salt
1 teaspoon pepper
1 cup light cream**

●

Heat the drippings in a skillet and stir in the flour. Simmer until brown and stir in the salt, pepper and light cream. Stir constantly over low heat until thick.

GLAZED CHICKEN WINGS

serves 6

24 chicken wings, trimmed
1 cup honey
¼ cup brandy
¼ cup soy sauce
2 garlic cloves, minced
1 teaspoon salt
1 teaspoon black pepper

•

Preheat the oven to 325°F. Rinse the wings and pat dry.

In a deep bowl, combine the honey, brandy, soy sauce, garlic, salt and pepper and blend thoroughly. Dip each wing into the glaze and place on a greased baking sheet.

Bake for 30 minutes, basting with the glaze and turning the wings every 5 minutes.

GARLIC-BAKED CHICKEN AND VEGETABLES

serves 6

¼ cup olive oil
3 garlic cloves, minced
6 chicken breasts, boneless and skinless
1 cup dry sherry
1 tablespoon lemon juice
1 teaspoon Worcestershire sauce
1 teaspoon salt
1 teaspoon cayenne pepper
1 red bell pepper, sliced into rings
1 green bell pepper, sliced into rings
1 red onion, sliced and pushed into rings
2 large tomatoes, chopped

•

Preheat the oven to 300°F. Heat the oil and garlic in a skillet and lightly brown the chicken. Transfer the chicken to paper towels to drain.

Add the sherry, lemon juice, Worcestershire sauce, salt and cayenne pepper to the skillet and simmer for 3 minutes. Put the red and green bell pepper rings in a large casserole dish and place the chicken on top of them. Top the chicken with the onion rings and chopped tomatoes. Pour the sauce over them, cover and bake for 45 minutes.

PARMESAN FRIED CHICKEN

serves 4

1 4-pound frying chicken, cut into
pieces
½ cup flour
½ cup cracker meal
½ cup grated Parmesan cheese
1½ teaspoons garlic powder
1½ teaspoons salt
1½ teaspoons cayenne pepper
vegetable oil or lard for frying

•

Rinse the chicken pieces and pat dry. Combine the flour, cracker meal, Parmesan cheese, garlic powder, salt and cayenne pepper in a large plastic bag and shake well.

Fill a deep heavy skillet with oil to a depth of 2 inches. Heat the oil over moderate heat until a drop of water sizzles when dropped into it.

Place a few of the chicken pieces in the bag and shake until well coated. Fry until golden brown on all sides, about 20 minutes, then drain on paper towels. Repeat with the remaining chicken.

ROAST CHICKEN WITH CHESTNUT AND RICE STUFFING

serves 8

1 onion, chopped
2 celery stalks with leaves, chopped
3 tablespoons butter
1½ teaspoons poultry seasoning
1 teaspoon salt
2 tablespoons chopped parsley
½ cup chopped uncooked chestnuts
½ cup chopped cooked giblets
2 cups slightly underdone rice
2 3-pound chickens
2 tablespoons French-style mustard
1 teaspoon salt
1 teaspoon black pepper
2 lemons

•

Preheat the oven to 375°F. Sauté the onions and celery in the butter and stir in the seasoning, salt, parsley, chestnuts and giblets. Continue to sauté for 5 minutes.

Blend the mixture with the rice in a large mixing bowl. Stuff the chickens with the stuffing and sew (or tie) closed. Rub the chickens with the mustard and sprinkle with the salt and pepper.

Place the chickens on a roasting pan with a rack and bake for 1½ hours. After the first 30 minutes squeeze the juice of one lemon over the chickens, and repeat with the remaining lemon after the second half hour.

SWEET CHICKEN

serves 4

1 4-pound chicken, cut into serving
pieces
½ teaspoon salt
½ teaspoon black pepper
¾ cup apple cider
½ cup orange juice
¼ cup lemon juice
1 onion, chopped
½ cup olive oil
2 apples, cored and sliced
½ cup seedless raisins
½ cup dried apricots
½ cup pitted prunes
4 tablespoons honey

●

Sprinkle salt and pepper on the
chicken pieces and place in a large
bowl. Cover with the apple cider,
lemon juice, orange juice and the
onion. Marinate for 1 hour.

Preheat the oven to 350°F. Remove
the chicken from the marinade and
reserve the marinade. Heat the olive
oil in a large skillet. Add the chicken
pieces and brown lightly.

Put the chicken in a large casserole
dish and cover with the apples,
raisins, apricots and prunes. Pour
the marinade over the casserole and
then pour the honey over the chicken
pieces. Bake, covered, for 45 minutes.

CHICKEN LIVERS IN COCONUT AND CHILI SAUCE

serves 6

1 chopped onion
2 garlic cloves, minced
8 dried red chili peppers
¼ cup unsalted cashew nuts
1 teaspoon shrimp paste
4 tablespoons vegetable oil
2 pounds chicken livers, soaked in cold
water for 1 hour
1 teaspoon salt
1 teaspoon sugar
½ teaspoon grated lemon peel
6 tablespoons chicken broth
½ cup coconut milk

●

Combine the onion, garlic, red
chilis, cashews and shrimp paste in
a blender and purée.

Heat the oil in a skillet and add the
puréed mixture. Stir constantly and
brown lightly. Stir in the drained
livers and brown. Stir in the salt,
sugar, lemon peel, broth and coconut milk, and bring to a boil. Reduce
the heat and simmer for 30 minutes.
Serve over rice.

BRANDIED DUCK

serves 4

1 4-pound duck
½ cup lemon juice
½ cup brandy
½ cup sweet butter, melted
¼ cup chopped parsley
1 teaspoon paprika

•

Preheat the oven to 375°F. Wash, rinse and dry the duck. Rub with the lemon juice.

Place the duck in a roasting pan and baste with a mixture of the brandy, butter and parsley. Sprinkle with the paprika and bake for 1½ hours, basting with the sauce every 15 minutes.

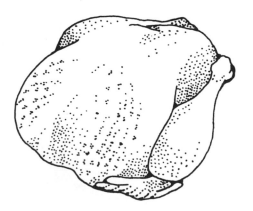

FRUIT-STUFFED GAME HENS WITH PLUM SAUCE

serves 6

1 pound seedless dried prunes,
coarsely chopped
6 Cornish game hens
¼ cup olive oil
3 apples, peeled, cored and diced
½ pound seedless grapes
1 cup bread cubes, no crusts
3 tablespoons chopped parsley
½ pound unsalted cashews, halved
½ cup dry sherry
2 teaspoons paprika
2 cups water
5 tablespoons sugar

•

Soak the prunes in a bowl filled with enough cold water to cover, for 2 hours.

Preheat the oven to 350°F. Rub the hens with the olive oil. Combine the apples, grapes, bread cubes, parsley, cashews and sherry in a mixing bowl and toss well. Stuff each hen with one-sixth of the mixture. Sprinkle with the paprika.

Place in a roasting pan and bake, uncovered, for 30 minutes. Cover and continue to bake for 1½ hours.

Drain the prunes, then combine them with the water and sugar in a saucepan and bring to a boil. Lower the heat and simmer for 1 hour, covered. Transfer the hens to a serving platter and spoon the sauce over them before serving.

LOUISIANA DUCK

serves 6

1 5-pound duck, cut into serving pieces
¼ cup brandy
1 cup dry red wine
1 large onion, chopped
1 tablespoon chopped parsley
3 tablespoons sweet butter, melted
3 tablespoons olive oil
2 garlic cloves, minced
¾ cup chicken broth
1 teaspoon salt
1 teaspoon cayenne pepper
1 teaspoon hot red-pepper sauce
½ teaspoon dried red pepper flakes
1 teaspoon oregano
1 teaspoon cinnamon
½ teaspoon nutmeg
1 tablespoon lemon juice

•

Arrange the duck pieces in a large casserole dish. Combine all the remaining ingredients in a large bowl. Mix well and pour over the duck. Refrigerate, covered, for 4 hours.

Preheat the oven to 350°F. Bake the duck for 1¼ hours, then remove the pieces from the sauce and place on a platter. Spoon some of the sauce over the pieces and serve.

HONEY DUCK

serves 6

4 pounds duck pieces
1 garlic clove, minced
1 teaspoon salt
2 cups mandarin orange sections, with liquid
¼ teaspoon ground ginger
¼ cup lemon juice
4 tablespoons honey
½ cup black cherries, pitted

•

Preheat the oven to 325°F. Place the duck pieces on a rack in a baking pan and bake, covered, for 1 hour.

Drain the pieces on paper towels and arrange in a casserole dish. Combine the garlic, salt, orange sections and liquid, ginger, lemon juice and honey in a bowl. Pour over the duck.

Bake, covered, for 30 minutes. Top with the cherries and bake, uncovered, for 10 minutes.

ROAST GOOSE

serves 8

1 10-pound goose
½ pound pitted prunes
1½ cups apple cider
5 apples, cored, peeled and sliced
½ cup slivered almonds
1 teaspoon grated orange rind
2 plums, seeded and chopped

•

Soak the prunes in the cider overnight.

Preheat the oven to 350°F. Rinse the goose inside and out and pat dry. Drain the prunes and reserve the cider.

Mix the prunes with the apples, almonds, orange rind and plums and stuff the goose. Sew closed. Bake in a large roasting pan for 3 hours, basting with the cider every 15 minutes.

SAUTÉED QUAIL

serves 6

¼ cup sweet butter
¼ cup olive oil
1 teaspoon salt
6 quail
1 cup white wine
½ teaspoon nutmeg
1 teaspoon white pepper
1 pound seedless white grapes
6 tablespoons brandy

•

Preheat the oven to 350°F. Melt the butter in a skillet and blend in the olive oil and salt. Place the quails in a roasting pan and brush with the mixture. Bake for 1 hour, basting every 10 minutes.

Remove the quails from the oven and pour the wine over them. Sprinkle each quail with some of the nutmeg and the white pepper. Surround the quail with the grapes.

Bake for 30 minutes and transfer to a serving platter. Use a slotted spoon to remove the grapes and place among the quail. Pour 1 tablespoon brandy over each quail and ignite. Serve.

NORTH CAROLINA TURKEY SOUSE

serves 8

3 pounds turkey pieces
1 cup cider vinegar
1 teaspoon dried red pepper flakes
1 teaspoon salt
½ teaspoon black pepper

•

Place the turkey pieces in a large pot with enough water to cover. Bring to a boil, reduce the heat and simmer until meat falls from bones.

Remove the meat and bones, reserving the liquid. Discard the bones and chop the meat very fine. Return the meat to the liquid and stir in the remaining ingredients.

Simmer uncovered for 30 minutes. Pour the mixture into a loaf pan and let set in refrigerator, covered, for 8 hours. Slice and serve with cornbread.

ROAST TURKEY WITH CORNBREAD STUFFING

serves 10

1 15-pound turkey
½ cup olive oil
2 tablespoons chopped parsley
1 tablespoon garlic powder
1 teaspoon salt
1 teaspoon black pepper
1 onion, chopped
3 celery stalks, chopped
3 teaspoons poultry seasoning
½ cup butter
4 cups unflavored breadcrumbs
4 cups cornbread crumbs
1 tablespoon chopped parsley
1 teaspoon oregano
¾ cup chicken broth

•

Rub the turkey with the olive oil, then rub a mixture of parsley, garlic powder, salt and pepper into the bird. Place in a large roasting pan and set aside.

Preheat the oven to 350°F. In a skillet, sauté the onion, celery and poultry seasoning in the butter. Mix the sautéed vegetables in a bowl with the breadcrumbs, cornbread crumbs, parsley, oregano and broth.

Stuff the bird with the mixture and sew or tie closed. Bake for 30 minutes uncovered then cover and bake for 4 hours. Do not stuff the bird in advance of cooking.

TURKEY GIBLET GRAVY

neck, liver, gizzard and heart of
1 large turkey
1 teaspoon salt
6 tablespoons water
½ cup flour
3 cups chicken broth

•

Place the giblets in a skillet and sprinkle with the salt. Add the water and bring to a boil. Lower the heat and simmer for 1 hour.

Discard the neck and finely chop the giblets. Melt the butter in the skillet and lightly brown the giblets. Stir in the flour and brown. Stir in the broth and bring to a boil.

Lower the heat and simmer, stirring, for 15 minutes or until the gravy is thick.

CORNFLAKE SCRAMBLE

serves 2

4 eggs
½ cup crumbled cornflakes
2 tablespoons milk
1½ teaspoons ketchup
½ teaspoon celery seeds
½ teaspoon salt
½ teaspoon black pepper
2 tablespoons butter

•

Beat the eggs in a bowl. Add the cornflakes, milk, ketchup, celery seeds, salt and pepper. Mix well.

Melt the butter in a skillet. Add the egg mixture and cook, stirring, until eggs are set. Serve hot.

GLAZED TURKEY DRUMSTICKS

serves 6

6 large turkey drumsticks
½ cup honey
½ cup dry sherry
1 teaspoon allspice
1 teaspoon nutmeg
1 teaspoon cinnamon
6 tablespoons brandy

•

Preheat the oven to 350°F. Rinse the drumsticks and pat dry.

Blend together the honey, sherry, allspice, nutmeg and cinnamon in a deep bowl. Dip each drumstick into the mixture and place in a greased baking dish.

Bake for 45 minutes, basting with the glaze and turning every 10 minutes. Put the drumsticks on a serving platter and pour 1 tablespoon of brandy over each. Ignite and serve.

CREOLE POACHED EGGS

serves 4

½ teaspoon hot red-pepper sauce
½ teaspoon salt
8 eggs
8 slices buttered toast

•

Fill a skillet with water to a depth of 1 inch. Add the hot red-pepper sauce and salt. Bring to a boil. Carefully break the eggs into the skillet and turn off the heat. When the eggs are set, transfer them with a slotted spoon, letting water drain back into the skillet onto the toast.

CREOLE OMELET

serves 4

1 large onion, finely chopped
2 tablespoons unflavored breadcrumbs
1 garlic clove, chopped
2 tablespoons butter
6 eggs
¼ pound ham, diced
3 tomatoes, seeded and coarsely
chopped
½ teaspoon salt
½ teaspoon black pepper
½ teaspoon cayenne pepper
2 tablespoons butter

•

Mix the onion with the breadcrumbs and garlic in a bowl. Melt the butter in a saucepan and sauté the onion mixture for 5 minutes.

Beat the eggs in a deep bowl and blend in the ham and tomatoes. Stir in the onion mixture, salt, pepper and cayenne pepper. Melt remaining butter in a large skillet until it is bubbling. Pour in the egg mixture and cook over medium heat until eggs are nearly set. Flip the omelet over, cook briefly on the other side, fold over and serve hot.

EGGS BENEDICTINE

serves 4

4 eggs
4 tablespoons cream
4 thin slices cooked ham
4 tomato slices
1 tablespoon butter
1 tablespoon flour
½ teaspoon salt
¼ teaspoon black pepper
1 cup milk
½ cup grated mild cheese
2 egg yolks, well beaten
½ cup dry sherry

•

Preheat the oven to 350°F. Place a tablespoon of cream, a slice of ham and a slice of tomato into each of four small oven proof dishes, then break one egg into each. Bake for 15 minutes, or until set.

While eggs are baking, melt the butter in a skillet and blend in the flour, salt and pepper. Blend in the milk and stir until thickened. Add the cheese and stir until the cheese melts. Remove from the heat and stir in the egg yolks and sherry. Pour the sauce over the baked eggs and serve at once.

FLORIDA EGG BAKE

serves 6

8 bacon strips
3 tablespoons flour
2 cups tomato purée
1 teaspoon salt
1 teaspoon black pepper
2 scallions, chopped
1 small red bell pepper, chopped
8 hard-cooked eggs, shelled and
quartered
¾ cup Monterey Jack cheese

•

Fry the bacon until almost crisp and drain on paper towels. Preheat the oven to 375°F. Pour off all but 3 tablespoons of the bacon drippings and stir in the flour. Blend well and sauté for 3 minutes. Stir in the tomato purée, salt and pepper and simmer for 15 minutes. Add the scallions and red bell pepper and continue to simmer for 5 minutes more.

Place the egg quarters in a buttered 1½-quart baking dish. Pour the sauce over the eggs and sprinkle with the cheese and crumbled bacon. Bake for 25 minutes and serve.

GULF-STYLE OMELET

serves 2

2 tablespoons butter
4 eggs
¼ cup chopped cooked shrimp
2 parsley sprigs
½ teaspoon cayenne pepper
¼ teaspoon hot red-pepper sauce
2 thick slices Munster cheese
1 chopped scallion
1 small chopped tomato

•

Melt the butter in a skillet. Combine the eggs, shrimp, parsley and cayenne pepper in a blender and process on low for 2 minutes. Pour the egg mixture into the skillet and add the hot red-pepper sauce.

As the eggs begin to set, lay the cheese slices on top, then sprinkle the scallion and tomato over them. As the bottom of the egg turns golden yellow, but before the top has completely set, fold the omelet. Cook for 2 minutes more and slide onto a serving platter.

LOUISIANA OMELET

serves 4

6 eggs, separated
2 teaspoons milk
2 tablespoons butter
3 cubes white sugar
1 cup dark rum

•

Beat the egg yolks in a bowl and blend in the milk. In a second bowl,

Hoppin' John

Baked Beans

Glazed Chicken Wings

beat the egg whites until they are stiff but not dry. Blend the two mixtures together.

Heat the butter in a skillet and pour in the egg mixture. Cook until the bottom is golden and it is almost set. Fold the omelet and place the sugar cubes on top. Pour over the rum and ignite. Keep spooning the rum over the omelet until the sugar has melted and the flame dies out.

NEW ORLEANS HERB OMELET

serves 2

4 eggs, very lightly beaten
4 tablespoons water
½ teaspoon salt
½ teaspoon black pepper
2 parsley sprigs, finely chopped
½ teaspoon chopped chives
1 teaspoon chopped watercress
½ teaspoon chopped chervil
2 tablespoons butter

•

Whisk together the eggs, water, salt, pepper and herbs in a bowl. Melt the butter in a skillet over medium heat and reduce the heat slightly when the butter is hot. Pour in the egg mixture and cook until lightly golden brown underneath and creamy on top. While cooking, gently lift the edges of the omelet to allow the uncooked part to run underneath. Fold and serve.

WHITE SAUCE

makes 1 cup

2 tablespoons butter
2 tablespoons flour
1 cup milk or light cream
½ teaspoon salt
¼ teaspoon white pepper
¼ teaspoon nutmeg

•

Melt the butter in a saucepan and stir in the flour. Stir until smooth and cook over low heat for 3 minutes. Do not brown. Stir the milk into the mixture and continue to cook over low heat, stirring constantly until bubbles appear. Blend in the salt, white pepper and nutmeg. Stir until thick.

KENTUCKY SCRAMBLE

serves 4

1 cup cooked corn
3 tablespoons bacon drippings
1 green bell pepper, chopped
1 tablespoon chopped parsley
1 tablespoon chopped pimento
6 eggs
1 teaspoon salt
½ teaspoon black pepper

•

Sauté the corn in the bacon drippings for 3 minutes. Stir in the bell pepper and sauté for 3 minutes. Stir in the parsley and pimento and sauté for 3 minutes.

Beat the eggs, salt and pepper together in a bowl and stir into the skillet. Scramble until set but still moist.

BEEF AND LAMB

ALEXANDER'S BEEF CHILI

serves 8

¼ cup butter
3 pounds cubed lean beef stew meat
2 garlic cloves, minced
2 tablespoons Worcestershire sauce
1 large onion, coarsely chopped
¼ cup shredded green chili peppers
3 tomatoes, coarsely chopped
¼ cup tomato paste
¼ cup white wine
¼ cup beef broth
1 teaspoon chili powder
1 teaspoon salt
1 teaspoon black pepper
½ teaspoon sugar

•

Melt the butter in a large skillet. Add the beef and brown on all sides. Stir in the garlic and Worcestershire sauce and simmer for 2 minutes. Stir in the onion and chili peppers and simmer for 5 minutes.

Stir in the tomatoes, tomato paste, wine, beef broth, chili powder, salt, pepper and sugar and bring to a boil. Reduce the heat and simmer for 45 minutes.

BEEF 'N' BISCUITS

serves 6

2 pounds cubed lean beef stew meat
½ cup flour
1 teaspoon salt
½ teaspoon black pepper
3 tablespoons bacon drippings
4 carrots, pared and sliced
1 large onion, cut into small wedges
6 potatoes, cut into wedges
2 cups stewed tomatoes, drained and juice reserved
1 herb bouquet (1 tablespoon each dried basil, chervil, marjoram and savory tied in a cheesecloth square)
12 buttermilk biscuits

•

Preheat the oven to 325°F.

Combine the flour, salt and pepper in a small bowl. Dredge the beef cubes in the flour mixture; reserve the leftover mixture. Heat the bacon drippings in a large skillet. Add the beef and brown on all sides. Remove the beef with a slotted spoon and place in a casserole dish. Add the carrots, onion, potatoes, drained tomatoes and herb bouquet.

Add the leftover flour mixture to the bacon drippings and blend thoroughly. Lightly brown and stir in the reserved tomato liquid. Simmer for 3 minutes. Pour the sauce over the meat and vegetables. Bake, covered for 3 hours. Serve over biscuits.

BAKED BEEFSTEAK

serves 4

4 ¾-pound steaks
3 tablespoons lemon juice
salt to taste
black pepper to taste
1 teaspoon garlic powder
1 large green bell pepper, sliced into
rings
1 onion, sliced into rings
1 cup water

•

Preheat the oven to 225°F. Sprinkle the lemon juice over the steaks. Sprinkle generously with the salt, pepper and garlic powder on both sides.

Arrange the steaks in a baking dish and cover with the green bell pepper rings and onion rings. Pour in the water and bake, tightly covered, for 2 hours.

BEEF IN BEER WITH LIMA BEANS

serves 6

4 tablespoons butter
2½ pounds cubed lean beef
1 garlic clove, minced
1 large onion, chopped
½ teaspoon thyme
½ teaspoon salt
½ teaspoon black pepper
12-ounces beer
2 cups fresh or thawed frozen small
lima beans

•

Melt the butter in a Dutch oven or heavy pot. Brown the meat on all sides. Stir in the garlic, onions, thyme, salt and pepper and simmer for 5 minutes.

Stir in the beer and simmer, covered, for 1 hour. Stir in the limas and simmer for another 30 minutes over medium-low heat. Serve over rice.

BEEF IN RED WINE

serves 6

¼ pound salt pork, diced
2 pounds cubed lean beef
1 large onion, chopped
1 garlic clove, minced
2 shallots, minced
1 carrot, julienned
1 tablespoon chopped parsley
6 black peppercorns
1 bay leaf
1 teaspoon tarragon
¼ teaspoon thyme
1 teaspoon salt
1 cup dry red wine

•

Sauté the salt pork in a large skillet until crisp. Remove with a slotted spoon and drain on paper towels.

Stir in the beef cubes and brown thoroughly on all sides. Remove with slotted spoon and drain on paper towels with the salt pork.

Stir in the beef cubes and brown thoroughly on all sides. Remove with a slotted spoon and drain on paper towels with the salt pork.
thyme, salt and red wine and bring to a boil. Reduce the heat to very low and simmer, covered, for 1½ hours. Stir in the salt pork and simmer for 15 minutes longer.

BEEF SCALLOPS

serves 6

2½ pounds beef rump, thinly sliced
½ cup flour
½ teaspoon salt
½ teaspoon black pepper
3 tablespoons butter
2 cups brown gravy
2 tablespoons butter
2 teaspoons cornstarch
1 tablespoon cold water
2 teaspoons salt
½ teaspoon cayenne pepper
3 scallions, chopped
4 small pickles, thinly sliced
1 teaspoon drained capers, finely chopped

•

Cut the beef slices in half. Place each slice between 2 sheets of waxed paper. Pound the slices flat with a mallet until they are very thin.

Combine the flour, salt and black pepper in a bowl. Dredge the slices in the flour mixture.

Melt the butter in a large heavy skillet. Add the beef scallops and fry for 2 minutes on each side.

Dissolve the cornstarch in the water in a small bowl. Add the gravy, butter, cornstarch, salt, cayenne pepper, scallions, pickles and capers to the skillet. Simmer over low heat for 1 hour. Serve over rice.

153

CHICKEN-FRIED STEAK WITH SPICY GRAVY

serves 6

**6 8-ounce steaks, about ½-inch thick
1½ teaspoons salt
½ teaspoon black pepper
flour
milk
vegetable shortening**

SPICY GRAVY:
**pan drippings from steaks
3 cups milk
6 tablespoons butter
¼ teaspoon cayenne pepper
¼ teaspoon hot red-pepper sauce
1½ teaspoons salt
½ cup flour**

•

Score the steaks crosswise on both sides with a sharp knife. Pound the steaks with a mallet until they are about ¼ inch thick.

Dust the steaks with the salt and pepper, then dredge each steak in the flour. Dip the coated steaks in the milk, and then dredge again in the flour.

Melt the shortening in a skillet over medium heat. Add the steaks and fry for 3 minutes (less for rare meat) on each side, pressing the steaks down on the skillet with a spatula from time to time. Remove the steaks when done and keep them warm.

To make the spicy gravy, heat the milk in a large saucepan over very low heat. Don't let the milk boil or form a skin

Reduce the heat under the skillet with the steak drippings. Add the butter, cayenne pepper, hot red-pepper sauce and salt. Stir for 1 minute. Slowly blend in the flour until the mixture is smooth. Slowly pour the mixture into the heated milk, stirring constantly so it blends evenly. Simmer the gravy (do not let it boil) until it thickens to taste. Serve in a gravy boat with the steaks.

JUICY ONION HAMBURGERS

serves 6

**2 pounds extra-lean ground beef
1 envelope dry onion soup mix
1 large egg, slightly beaten
6 large buns, buttered**

•

Preheat the broiler. If the oven is a separate unit, preheat at the lowest setting.

Combine the beef, onion soup mix and egg in a bowl and blend thoroughly. Form the mixture into 6 thick patties. Place the patties on a broiler pan with a rack and broil for 5 minutes. Turn the burgers and broil for 4 minutes longer. Warm the buns in the oven. After the third minute, turn off the broiler and remove the buns from the oven. Place the buns, open-face, on plates. Remove the burgers from the broiler and give each one a squeeze with a spatula before transferring to the buns. Serve immediately.

CREOLE GRILLADES

serves 4 to 6

1 to 1½ pounds beef round,
approximately ½-inch thick
salt to taste
black pepper to taste
⅛ teaspoon cayenne pepper
2 tablespoons lard or olive oil
1 small onion, thinly sliced
2 garlic cloves, finely chopped
1 large tomato, chopped

•

Trim the fat from the meat. Cut it into 3- or 4-inch squares. Place the meat squares between two sheets of waxed paper. Using a mallet, pound the squares until they are about ¼-inch thick. Rub the meat on both sides with salt, pepper and cayenne pepper.

In a large, heavy skillet heat the lard. Add the onion and garlic and sauté, stirring constantly, until brown, about 5 to 7 minutes. Stir in the tomato and cook for 2 minutes.

Add the meat and stir well to coat on all sides. Cover the skillet and cook for 10 minutes, or until the beef is tender and well browned. Serve hot with beans or rice.

MARINATED RIB-EYE STEAKS

serves 6

6 8-ounce rib-eye steaks
2 tablespoons olive oil
salt to taste
black pepper to taste
4 tablespoons chili sauce
2 tablespoons lemon juice
1 tablespoon red wine vinegar
2 tablespoons white wine
1 teaspoon sugar

•

Rub the steaks with the olive oil and salt and pepper. Let stand for 10 minutes. Preheat the broiler. Combine the chili sauce, lemon juice, vinegar, wine and sugar in a small saucepan. Simmer, stirring constantly, for 5 minutes.

Place the steaks on a broiler pan with a rack and brush with half the marinade. Place under the broiler and cook for 5 minutes. Turn the steaks and brush with the remaining marinade. Broil for 4 minutes longer and serve.

MARINATED SHORT RIBS

serves 6

¼ cup olive oil
¼ cup white wine
2 tablespoons lemon juice
2 garlic cloves, minced
1 tablespoon chopped parsley
1 teaspoon salt
½ teaspoon black pepper
½ teaspoon cayenne pepper
6 pounds beef short ribs

●

Combine the olive oil, white wine, lemon juice, garlic, parsley, salt, pepper and cayenne pepper in a blender. Process on low speed for 1 minute. Place the ribs in a deep dish and pour the marinade over them. Cover the dish and refrigerate for 8 to 12 hours.

Remove the ribs from the refrigerator and let stand for 1 hour. Preheat the oven to 350°F. Place the ribs in a roasting pan and cover with aluminum foil. Bake for 30 minutes and pour off fat. Brush the ribs with the marinade and bake, uncovered, for 1 hour, brushing with the marinade every 10 minutes.

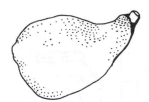

MEAT BALLS

serves 6

2 pounds lean ground beef
½ cup cracker meal
2 eggs, slightly beaten
1 tablespoon chopped parsley
½ teaspoon cumin
½ teaspoon salt
½ teaspoon white pepper
¼ cup vegetable oil
¼ cup cornmeal
¼ cup sifted flour

●

In a large mixing bowl, combine the meat, cracker meal, eggs, parsley, cumin, salt and pepper. Blend thoroughly. Form the meat mixture into balls and dredge in a mixture of cornmeal and flour.

Heat the oil in a skillet over medium heat. Fry the meat balls for 4 minutes on the first side, turn over and continue cooking for 3 minutes longer. Drain on paper towels.

Meat Loaf

serves 8

2½ pounds lean ground beef
½ cup cracker meal
1 large onion, chopped
2 tablespoons chopped pimento
2 eggs, slightly beaten
2 tablespoons chopped parsley
½ teaspoon salt
½ teaspoon thyme
4 orange slices
¼ cup tomato paste
2 tablespoons cider vinegar
3 tablespoons orange juice
½ teaspoon salt
½ teaspoon sugar

•

Preheat the oven to 350°F. Combine the meat, cracker meal, onion, pimento, eggs, parsley, salt and thyme in a large mixing bowl and blend thoroughly. Pack the mixture tightly in a lightly buttered loaf pan. Turn the loaf out of the loaf pan into a roasting pan and bake for 1 hour, with the orange slices placed on top of the loaf.

Combine the tomato paste, cider vinegar, orange juice, salt and sugar in a saucepan and blend thoroughly. Cook over medium heat and simmer, stirring constantly, for 5 minutes. Reduce the heat to very low and simmer for 5 minutes more.

After the loaf has been cooking for 20 minutes, baste with some of the sauce. Baste twice again at 15-minute intervals. With 2 spatulas, carefully lift the loaf from the pan, allowing any drippings to drain back into the pan, and place on a platter for serving.

Southern-Style Pot Roast

serves 6

1 3-pound beef round or rump roast
½ teaspoon salt
½ teaspoon black pepper
1 tablespoon brown sugar
2 tablespoons butter
2 tablespoons olive oil
1 large onion, chopped
1 tablespoon tomato paste
¼ teaspoon ground cloves
1 cup water
4 white potatoes, cut into wedges
8 pearl onions
4 carrots, julienned

•

Rub the roast with a mixture of the salt, pepper and brown sugar.

Melt the butter in a large pot and blend in the oil. Brown the roast on all sides. Remove the meat to a platter and add the onions to the pot. Sauté for 5 minutes. Stir in the tomato paste, water, cloves, potatoes, onions and carrots.

Move the vegetables to the sides of the pot and put the meat back in. Arrange the vegetables around the meat. Cover tightly and simmer for 2 hours over low heat.

OPEN-FACED SLOPPY JOES

serves 8

3 tablespoons butter
1 onion, chopped
2½ pounds extra-lean ground beef
2 garlic cloves, minced
1 tablespoon Worcestershire sauce
4 tablespoons tomato paste
4 tablespoons white wine
½ teaspoon salt
½ teaspoon cayenne pepper
½ teaspoon sugar
8 large buns, lightly buttered

•

Melt the butter in a skillet and sauté the onions for 5 minutes. Stir in the beef and brown. Preheat the broiler. Pour off most of the liquid from the skillet and add the garlic and Worcestershire sauce. Stir and simmer for 2 minutes. Stir in the tomato paste, white wine, salt, cayenne pepper and sugar and simmer for 5 minutes, stirring constantly.

Place the buns in an oven-proof dish. Spoon equal portions of the meat mixture on each half. Place under the broiler for 2 minutes. Serve immediately.

ROAST BEEF

serves 10 with enough left over for sandwiches

1 10-pound boneless beef rib roast
4 garlic cloves, halved
¼ cup olive oil
4 tablespoons oregano
4 tablespoons chopped parsley
2 teaspoons salt
1 teaspoon black pepper
1 tablespoon poppy seeds
2 teaspoons paprika
½ cup white wine
¼ cup lemon juice
2 tablespoons Worcestershire sauce

•

Preheat the oven to 500°F. Trim off excess fat from the roast and place in a large roasting pan. Cut 8 slits in the top of the roast with a sharp knife and stuff each with a garlic clove half. Rub the roast with half the oil and place in the oven, uncovered, for 10 minutes.

Remove from the oven, reduce the heat to 325°F, and allow the roast to cool slightly. Brush the roast with the remaining oil and rub a mixture of the oregano and parsley all over the roast. Sprinkle the roast with the salt, pepper, poppy seeds and paprika. Combine the wine, lemon juice and Worcestershire sauce in a small bowl and blend well. Pour the liquid around the roast, then using aluminum foil, form an enclosed tent over the roast. Be careful not to let the foil rest on the roast.

Bake for 3 hours and remove the garlic as you slice the roast.

SOUTHERN-STYLE BEEF GOULASH

serves 6

¼ cup butter
3 pounds cubed beef stew meat
2 onions, chopped
1 garlic cloved, minced
1 tablespoon paprika
1½ teaspoons salt
1 cup beef broth
3 tablespoons dry white wine
2 tablespoons flour
3 tablespoons water
1 cup sour cream

•

Melt the butter in a large skillet and stir in the beef, onions, and garlic. Brown well. Sprinkle the paprika and salt over the meat, and pour in the beef broth and wine. Stir and bring liquid to a boil. Reduce the heat and simmer, covered, for 40 minutes.

Blend together the flour and water in a small bowl. Stir into the skillet. Simmer for 10 minutes, remove from the heat and stir in the sour cream. Serve immediately over buttered noodles.

STEAK SMOTHERED IN ONIONS

serves 4

4 tablespoons butter
2 large onions, sliced and broken
into rings
1 teaspoon chopped parsley
1 garlic clove, minced
½ teaspoon salt
1 tablespoon flour
4 8-ounce filets mignon
½ cup beef broth

•

Melt the butter in a large skillet and stir in the onion rings, parsley, garlic and salt. Sauté until onions are golden. Stir in flour and lightly brown. Push the onions to the sides of the pan and add the filets. Thoroughly brown on all sides.

Stir in the broth and bring to a boil. Lower the heat and simmer for 10 minutes, or until most of the liquid is gone.

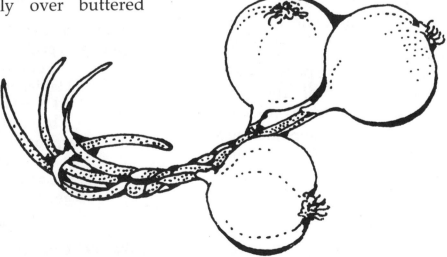

STUFFED PEPPERS

serves 6

6 large green bell peppers
1 pound lean ground beef
3 tablespoons olive oil
1 cup underdone rice
2 tablespoons chopped parsley
2 tablespoons chopped pimentos
1 celery stalk, finely chopped
¼ cup white wine
1 egg, slightly beaten
3 tablespoons lemon juice
1 tablespoon Worcestershire sauce

•

Remove the tops and seeds from the peppers. Blanch the peppers in a large pot of boiling water for 10 minutes. Drain well. Preheat the oven to 325°F.

Heat 1 tablespoon of the olive oil in a large skillet. Add the ground beef and sauté until browned. Drain off the fat.

Stir in the rice, pimentos and celery and sauté for 2 minutes.

Remove the skillet from the heat and transfer the mixture to a mixing bowl. Blend in the wine and egg. Stuff the peppers with the mixture.

Rub the outsides of the peppers with the remaining olive oil and place them in a roasting pan. Sprinkle the lemon juice and Worcestershire sauce over the peppers. Bake for 20 minutes and serve.

BREADED VEAL CUTLETS

serves 6

¼ cup cracker meal
¼ cup flour, sifted
2 tablespoons grated Parmesan cheese
1 tablespoon chopped parsley
½ teaspoon garlic powder
½ teaspoon salt
1 large egg, beaten
¼ cup olive oil
6 8-ounce veal cutlets

•

Combine the cracker meal, flour, Parmesan cheese, parsley, garlic powder and salt in a bowl, and blend thoroughly. Beat the egg in another bowl. Dip the veal cutlets in the egg and dredge in the flour mixture.

Heat the olive oil in a skillet over moderate heat. Fry the cutlets for 4 minutes on each side and drain on paper towels.

CORNED BEEF HASH

serves 4

1 pound cooked corned beef, shredded
2 potatoes, peeled and coarsely grated
1 onion, grated
2 tablespoons butter
1 cup beef broth
1 bay leaf, crushed
1 teaspoon chopped parsley
½ teaspoon salt
½ teaspoon black pepper
½ teaspoon cayenne pepper

•

Mix the corned beef and potatoes together. Sauté the onion in the butter over low heat. Stir in the meat and potatoes and sauté over medium heat for 3 minutes.

Stir in the broth, bay leaf, parsley, salt, pepper, and cayenne pepper and bring to a boil. Reduce heat and simmer for 20 minutes, or until almost all the liquid is absorbed.

KIDNEYS À LA FRANÇAISE

serves 4

**2 beef kidneys
8 tablespoons flour
4 tablespoons bacon drippings
2 cups boiling water
1 bay leaf
1 teaspoon salt
½ teaspoon cayenne pepper
1 lemon slice**

•

Soak the kidneys in a large bowl of cold water for 1 hour, changing the water 3 times. Drain well and place in a saucepan. Cover with fresh water and bring to a boil. Drain, cover with fresh water and bring to a boil again. Drain and cool.

Cut the cord and center fat from each kidney. Thinly slice the kidneys. Dredge the slices in 4 tablespoons of the flour. Heat the bacon drippings in a large, heavy skillet and fry the slices for 2 to 3 minutes per side. Drain on paper towels.

Stir in the remaining flour and blend with the drippings. Fry, stirring con-

stantly, until flour is brown. Stir in the water, bay leaf, salt, cayenne pepper and lemon slice and blend well. Add the kidney slices and simmer over low heat for 1 hour. Serve over rice.

LIVER WITH CREAMED GRAVY

serves 4

**4 strips bacon
1½ pounds beef or calves' liver, thinly sliced
¼ cup flour
½ teaspoon salt
¼ teaspoon black pepper
1 onion, chopped
½ cup light cream**

•

Fry the bacon in a skillet until crisp and drain on paper towels. Crumble the bacon and set aside.

Dredge the liver slices in a mixture of the flour, salt and pepper and fry for 5 minutes on one side. Turn the liver slices over and add the onions around, but not on top of, them. Simmer for 5 minutes more and remove the liver to drain on paper towels.

Add crumbled bacon to the onions and stir well. Blend in the cream and simmer, stirring, for 5 minutes, or until gravy thickens. Serve the liver with rice and pour the gravy over both.

MARINATED VEAL

serves 6

2 pounds veal cutlets, thinly sliced
¼ cup olive oil
¼ cup lemon juice
2 tablespoons soy sauce
1 tablespoon red wine
1 tablespoon Worcestershire sauce
1 teaspoon oregano
½ teaspoon salt
¼ teaspoon black pepper
1 tablespoon chopped parsley

•

Place the veal cutlets between sheets of waxed paper. Flatten with a mallet until very thin. Place the cutlets in a large bowl.

Combine the olive oil, lemon juice, soy sauce, Worcestershire sauce, oregano, salt, pepper and parsley in a blender. Process on low for 2 minutes. Pour the marinade over the veal. Cover and refrigerate for 2 hours.

Heat a dry skillet until very hot. Cook the cutlets for 2 minutes on each side.

ROAST VEAL CAJUN

serves 8

1 4-pound veal loin
3 tablespoons lemon juice
2 mint sprigs, finely chopped
2 garlic cloves, minced
2 teaspoons cayenne pepper
¼ cup olive oil

•

Sprinkle the lemon juice over the veal and rub in the mint, garlic and cayenne pepper. Allow to stand for 1 hour.

Preheat the oven to 375°F. Heat the olive oil in a large skillet and lightly brown the meat on all sides. Lift from the skillet and allow any excess oil to run off. Place the meat in a baking pan, cover and bake for 1 to 1¼ hours.

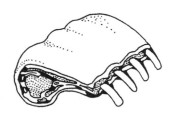

LAMB CURRY

serves 6

¼ cup olive oil
1 teaspoon curry powder
2 pounds cubed boneless lamb
1 onion, chopped
½ cup white wine
¼ cup brandy
2 celery stalks, chopped
2 carrots, chopped
2 tablespoons chopped parsley
1 teaspoon salt
1 teaspoon cayenne pepper
2 garlic cloves, minced
2 tablespoons melted butter
2 tablespoons sifted flour
½ cup heavy cream

•

Heat the oil in a large, heavy skillet and blend in the curry. Add the lamb and brown well on all sides.

Add the onions and sauté for 5 minutes over moderate heat. Stir in the white wine, brandy, celery, carrots, parsley, salt, cayenne pepper and garlic and bring to a boil. Stir in the butter, flour and heavy cream and reduce the heat to low. Simmer for 45 minutes, stirring occasionally. Serve with rice.

CROWN ROAST OF LAMB

serves 6

1 12-chop crown roast of lamb
¼ cup olive oil
1 tablespoon chopped parsley
2 garlic cloves, minced
1 tablespoon dried mint
rice pilaf

•

Purchase a 12-chop rack of lamb from the butcher and have him form the crown. Preheat the oven to 300°F.

Rub the meat with the olive oil and then rub with the parsley, garlic and mint. Stuff the inside of the crown with crumpled aluminum foil to help the crown keep its shape during cooking. Wrap the tips of the chops with foil. Carefully place the crown on a roasting pan with a rack. Roast for 1½ hours.

Prepare the rice. Remove the lamb from the oven and transfer to a platter. Remove the foil from the center of the crown and fill with the rice. Serve garnished with parsley sprigs and wedges of lemon.

LAMB SHANKS

serves 6

6 8-ounce lamb shanks
1 large egg, slightly beaten
1 cup fine unflavored breadcrumbs
1 tablespoon finely chopped parsley
¼ teaspoon thyme
¼ teaspoon marjoram
¼ teaspoon savory
½ teaspoon salt
¼ teaspoon grated lemon rind
4 tablespoons butter
4 tablespoons dry sherry

•

Combine the breadcrumbs, parsley, thyme, marjoram, savory, salt and lemon rind in a bowl. Mix well. Dip the lamb shanks in the beaten egg and then dredge in the breadcrumb mixture.

Melt the butter in a large skillet. Add the shanks and brown well on all sides. Cover and cook for 10 minutes. Remove the shanks to a platter and stir the sherry into the skillet. Blend thoroughly and simmer for 5 minutes. Pour the sauce over the shanks and serve.

LAMB-STUFFED TOMATOES

serves 8

8 large tomatoes
1 pound cooked chopped lamb meat
2 cups underdone rice
½ cup cooked chopped shrimp
2 teaspoons crushed dried mint
6 tablespoons lemon juice

•

Preheat the oven to 300°F. Remove the tops of the tomatoes and scoop out the meat and seeds. Reserve and chop the meat of 2 tomatoes. Discard the rest.

Mix the tomato meat, lamb, rice, shrimp and mint flakes in a bowl. Stuff the tomatoes with the mixture.

Place the tomatoes in a greased roasting pan and sprinkle with 3 tablespoons lemon juice. Bake for 20 minutes. Sprinkle the remaining lemon juice over the tomatoes. Bake for 15 minutes more and serve.

Green Beans and Bacon

Sweet Potato Pie

Crab Casserole

VEAL WITH GARLIC, TOMATOES AND SCALLIONS

serves 6

2 pounds veal cutlets, thinly sliced
into strips
¼ cup butter
3 garlic cloves, minced
2 tablespoons lemon juice
½ teaspoon oregano
½ teaspoon cayenne pepper
6 plum tomatoes, chopped
6 scallions, chopped
½ cup white wine
½ cup light cream
1 tablespoon flour
1 tablespoon chopped parsley
½ teaspoon salt

•

Lightly brown the veal strips in the
butter in a large skillet. Stir in the
garlic. Sauté for 3 minutes, stirring
constantly. Stir in the lemon juice,
oregano, cayenne pepper, tomatoes
and onion, and sauté for 5 minutes,
stirring constantly. Add the wine
and cream and bring almost to a boil.
Stir in the flour, parsley and salt and
simmer over low heat for 10 minutes.
Serve with rice.

LAMB CHOPS IN WINE SAUCE

serves 6

6 thick lamb chops
½ teaspoon salt
½ teaspoon black pepper
3 tablespoons butter
2 tablespoons French-style mustard
1 16-ounce can celery hearts, reserving
the liquid
1 cup tomato juice
½ cup dry white wine
¼ cup chopped parsley

•

Sprinkle the chops with the salt and
pepper. Melt the butter in a large
skillet. Add the chops and brown
well on both sides. Spread the
mustard over the chops. Add the
celery hearts, reserved celery liquid,
tomato juice and wine. Cover and
simmer over low heat for 1 hour.

Transfer the chops to a serving platter and keep warm. Pour the skillet
liquids into a blender and blend on
low for 2 minutes.

Return the sauce to the skillet and
heat until it bubbles and thickens,
stirring constantly. Spoon sauce over
the chops and sprinkle with the
parsley before serving.

MINT JULEP CHOPS

serves 6

6 thick lamb chops
1 tablespoon crushed dried mint
½ teaspoon salt
½ teaspoon black pepper
1 tablespoon butter
6 canned pineapple rings, drained
6 teaspoons bourbon whiskey

•

Preheat the broiler. Rub the chops with the mint, salt and pepper. Place the chops on a broiler pan with a rack and broil for 8 minutes. Turn the chops and cook for 8 minutes more.

While the chops cook, melt the butter in a skillet. Add the pineapple rings and lightly brown on both sides. Remove the chops from the broiler and transfer them to a platter. Top each with a pineapple ring and pour 1 teaspoon of bourbon whiskey over each. Ignite the whiskey and serve.

SAUTÉED LAMB KIDNEYS

serves 6

½ cup butter
1 garlic clove, minced
12 lamb kidneys, halved and trimmed
½ pound fresh mushrooms, trimmed and quartered
1 onion, halved and sliced
½ teaspoon salt
½ teaspoon black pepper
4 tablespoons lemon juice
1 tablespoon crushed rosemary
4 tablespoons white wine

•

Heat the butter and garlic in a skillet. Add the kidneys and brown lightly on all sides. Stir in the mushrooms and onion and sauté for 5 minutes.

Stir in the salt, pepper, lemon juice, rosemary and wine. Simmer for 10 minutes over low heat. Serve over rice.

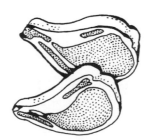

Mint-Stuffed Barbecued Lamb

serves 8

1 7-pound leg of lamb, boned
2 cups fresh mint leaves
1½ cups cider vinegar
½ cup butter
1 tablespoon Worcestershire sauce
½ teaspoon hot red pepper flakes
2 garlic cloves, minced
2 tablespoons lemon juice

•

Stuff the leg of lamb with the mint leaves and tie the leg closed. Wrap in foil and refrigerate overnight. Remove from the refrigerator 1 hour before cooking. Combine the vinegar, butter, Worcestershire sauce, red pepper flakes, garlic and lemon juice in a saucepan and bring to a quick boil. Lower the heat and simmer for 20 minutes. Start the coals in the grill.

Remove the foil from the lamb and skewer it securely on a long metal skewer from grill. Place the leg on a spit and cook for 2 hours, brushing with the sauce often.

Roast Leg of Lamb

serves 8

1 10-pound leg of lamb, trimmed
4 garlic cloves, halved
¼ cup olive oil
2 tablespoons chopped parsley
2 tablespoons mint flakes
1 teaspoon cayenne pepper
1 teaspoon salt
1 teaspoon paprika
2 cups white wine
½ cup lemon juice
¼ cup Worcestershire sauce

•

Preheat the oven to 375°F. Cut 8 slits into the lamb with a sharp knife and fill each with a garlic clove half. Put the lamb in a roasting pan and rub with the olive oil, parsley, mint, cayenne pepper, salt and paprika. Roast in the oven for 30 minutes, uncovered.

Remove from the oven and allow to cool slightly. Using aluminum foil, form an enclosed tent over the leg, being careful not to let the foil rest on the meat. Cut a 2-inch slit along the edge of the foil on one side of the pan.

Blend together the wine, lemon juice and Worcestershire sauce in a bowl. Pour ¾ cup of the mixture through the slit into the pan. Roast for 3½ hours, adding 1 cup of the wine mixture at the end of the first hour and the remainder at the end of the second hour.

STUFFED LAMB BREASTS

serves 8

5 strips bacon
1 small onion, chopped
6 cups bread cubes, crusts removed
⅓ cup chopped cooked shrimp
3 tablespoons chopped parsley
1 teaspoon basil
½ teaspoon salt
½ teaspoon black pepper
3 eggs, beaten
½ cup light cream
2 tablespoons olive oil
2 2½-pound lamb breasts, with pockets
BROWN SAUCE:
1½ cups bouillon
1 teaspoon dry mustard
1 teaspoon Worcestershire sauce
1 teaspoon steak sauce
½ teaspoon celery seeds
1 bay leaf
2 whole cloves
1 onion, halved

●

Preheat the oven to 350°F. Fry the bacon until crisp in a large skillet and drain on paper towels. Crumble the bacon. Add the onions to the bacon drippings and sauté for 3 minutes.

In a mixing bowl, combine the onion, crumbled bacon, bread cubes, shrimp, parsley, basil, salt and pepper and toss well.

In another bowl mix the eggs and cream. Add to the stuffing mixture. Stuff the lamb breasts and rub the outside of the meat with the olive oil. Place the breasts in a large baking pan and bake for 20 minutes.

In a saucepan, combine all the brown sauce ingredients and bring to a boil. Lower the heat and simmer for 15 minutes. Transfer an onion half to the top of each lamb breast and baste with brown sauce. Bake the breasts for 2 hours, basting every 15 minutes with the brown sauce.

PORK

BARBECUED CHOPPED HAM

serves 6

2 tablespoons butter
2 pounds lean ham, chopped
2 tablespoons chopped pimento
2 tablespoons crushed pineapple
½ teaspoon cayenne pepper
¼ cup chili sauce
1 tablespoon lemon juice
3 tablespoons brown sugar
3 tablespoons water

•

Melt the butter in a skillet. Add the ham, pimento and pineapple and cook until ham is browned.

Stir in the cayenne pepper, chili sauce, lemon juice, brown sugar and water and bring to a boil. Lower the heat and simmer for 20 minutes. Serve over rice.

BARBECUED PORK SANDWICHES

serves 8

4 tablespoons olive oil
2½ pounds lean pork, cut into small cubes
2 garlic cloves, minced
1 jalapeño pepper, seeded and chopped
6 ounces tomato paste
¾ cup white wine
½ teaspoon salt
½ teaspoon cayenne pepper
½ teaspoon chili powder
1 tablespoon Worcestershire sauce
1 tablespoon cider vinegar
1 teaspoon sugar
1 tablespoon molasses
8 large buns
butter

•

Heat the oil in a deep skillet. Add the meat and brown thoroughly on all sides. Stir in the garlic and pepper. Simmer for 5 minutes, stirring constantly. Stir in the tomato paste, wine, salt, cayenne, chili powder, sugar, Worcestershire sauce, vinegar and molasses.

Bring the mixture to a boil and lower the heat. Simmer, stirring occasionally, for 30 minutes.

Heat a large skillet or griddle. Butter each half bun and place on the griddle. Toast for 2 to 3 minutes, until the buttered side of each bun is golden brown. Spoon equal portions of the pork onto each bun and serve.

BOILED HAM

serves 10, with more for sandwiches

**1 6-pound boneless ham
2 blades mace
12 whole cloves
3 bay leaves
1 tablespoon black peppercorns**

•

Scrub and rinse the ham and place it in a large roasting pan. Cover with water and add the mace, cloves, bay leaves and peppercorns.

Place the roasting pan over two burners on the stove, uncovered, and bring to a very slow boil. Simmer 2 hours, skimming off foam every 30 minutes.

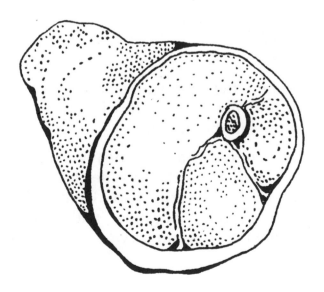

BRAISED PORK IN RED WINE SAUCE

serves 8

**1 4-pound pork tenderloin
3 cups dry red wine
2 large onions, chopped
1 carrot, coarsely chopped
2 garlic cloves, minced
1½ tablespoons tarragon vinegar
½ teaspoon black peppercorns
3 whole cloves
1½ teaspoons salt
2 tablespoons bacon drippings
⅓ cup currant jelly
1½ teaspoons grated lemon rind**

•

Lightly score the tenderloin with a knife. In a mixing bowl, combine the wine, onions, carrots, garlic, vinegar, peppercorns, cloves and salt. Place the tenderloin in a large deep dish and pour the marinade over it. Cover and refrigerate for 2 days.

Remove the meat from the marinade and drain well, reserving the marinade. Preheat the oven to 325°F.

Heat the bacon drippings over medium heat in a large skillet. Quickly brown the meat on all sides. Pour the marinade in a saucepan. Add the currant jelly and grated lemon rind and bring to a boil, stirring often. Place the tenderloin in a large casserole dish and pour the marinade over it. Cover the dish and bake for 2 hours.

BARBECUED SPARERIBS

serves 8

8 pounds pork spareribs
½ cup cider vinegar
1 cup water
4 tablespoons brown sugar
2 tablespoons dry mustard
1 tablespoon salt
1 teaspoon cayenne pepper
8 tablespoons lemon juice
2 onions, chopped
1 cup ketchup
4 tablespoons Worcestershire sauce
4 tablespoons butter
1 tablespoon liquid smoke
1 cup drained crushed pineapple

•

Preheat the oven to 425°F. Place the ribs in a large roasting pan in one layer and cover with foil. Bake for 45 minutes.

Combine the vinegar, water, brown sugar, mustard, salt, cayenne pepper, lemon juice, onions and ketchup in a saucepan and bring to a boil. Reduce the heat and simmer for 20 minutes. Stir in the Worcestershire sauce, butter, liquid smoke and pineapple. Continue to simmer over very low heat.

When the ribs have cooked, remove them from the oven and lower the temperature to 350°F. Remove the foil and drain off half the pan drippings. Pour half the sauce over the ribs and bake, uncovered, for 1 hour, basting every 10 minutes with the remaining sauce.

CHITTLINS

serves 4

1½ pounds fresh chittlins (pig intestine)
cold water
1 tablespoon lemon juice
½ cup cornmeal
½ cup cracker meal
½ teaspoon salt
½ teaspoon black pepper
1 cup vegetable oil for frying
1 onion, chopped

•

Place the chittlins in a bowl and cover with cold water mixed with 1 tablespoon lemon juice. Soak for 2 hours.

Drain the chittlins well. Cut them down their length and turn them inside out. Thoroughly clean and rinse the chitlins. Cut them into 2-inch pieces.

Combine the cornmeal, cracker meal, salt and pepper in a bowl. Roll the chittlins in the mixture.

Heat the oil in a large heavy skillet over medium heat. Add the chittlins and fry until very crisp. Drain on paper towels. Sprinkle with the chopped onions and serve.

CREOLE ROAST PORK

serves 8

1 6-pound pork loin roast
1 teaspoon salt
½ teaspoon black pepper
1 teaspoon dried sage
8 large apples, cored
4 sweet potatoes, cooked, peeled and mashed
2 tablespoons brown sugar
1 teaspoon lemon juice
¼ teaspoon grated nutmeg
¼ cup melted butter
¼ cup pure maple syrup

•

Preheat the oven to 300°F. Rub the salt, pepper and sage into the meat. Place the roast on a rack in a baking pan and roast for 3 hours, covered.

Using a sharp knife, remove enough pulp from the inside of the apples to make the opening 1½ inches wide. Chop the removed pulp and blend with the mashed sweet potatoes, brown sugar, lemon juice and nutmeg. In a small saucepan, simmer the butter and maple syrup for 2 minutes. Brush the insides of the apples with a little of this mixture. Stuff the apples with the mashed sweet potato mixture.

Remove the roast from the oven and drain off all pan liquids. Surround the roast with the stuffed apples.

Pour the remaining butter sauce over the pork and apples. Cover and bake for 30 minutes longer.

GLAZED PORK AND HAM LOAF

serves 8

2 pounds ground ham
1½ pounds ground lean pork
1 teaspoon salt
½ teaspoon black pepper
2 eggs, beaten
1 cup light cream
1 cup cracker crumbs
1½ cups firmly packed brown sugar
1 tablespoon French-style mustard
½ cup cider vinegar
½ cup water
1 tablespoon lemon juice

•

Preheat the oven to 350°F. In a large mixing bowl combine the ham, pork, salt, pepper, eggs, light cream and cracker crumbs. Fill a loaf pan and pack firmly with this mixture. Bake for 1½ hours.

Combine the brown sugar, mustard, cider vinegar, water and lemon juice in a saucepan and blend well. Bring almost to a boil, lower heat and simmer for 10 minutes. After the loaf has baked for 30 minutes, baste the top with the glaze every 10 minutes.

Allow to cool slightly before serving.

FRIED PORK CHOPS

serves 6

6 thick pork chops
2 tablespoons lemon juice
½ cup vegetable oil for frying
¼ cup cracker meal
¼ cup flour, sifted
¼ cup grated Parmesan cheese
1 tablespoon finely chopped parsley
½ teaspoon garlic powder
½ teaspoon salt

•

Sprinkle the lemon juice over the chops and let stand for 10 minutes.

Place the oil in a skillet over medium heat.

Combine the cracker meal, flour, cheese, parsley, garlic and salt in a bowl. Dredge the pork chops in the mixture and place in the skillet.

Cook for 8 minutes, carefully turn and cook for 8 minutes more. Drain on paper towels.

HAM MOUSSE

serves 6

2 eggs, separated
2 envelopes unflavored gelatin
¼ cup dry sherry
1⅓ cups chicken broth
3½ cups ground ham
1 cup heavy cream

•

Beat the egg whites in a bowl until stiff. Beat the cream in another bowl until it forms soft peaks. Sprinkle gelatin over the sherry in a bowl to soften and let stand. In a saucepan, heat the chicken broth until it bubbles. Beat the yolks slightly in a bowl, stir in 2 tablespoons of the broth and pour into the saucepan. Cook over low heat, stirring constantly, for 2 minutes.

Remove from the heat and stir in the sherry/gelatin mix. Blend in the ham. Fold in the beaten egg whites and cream.

Turn into a 1-quart mold and refrigerate until firm. Unmold on a platter and surround with parsley.

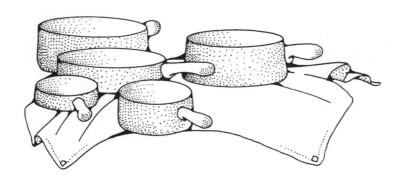

HAMSTEAK QUICHE

serves 6 to 8

6 strips bacon, chopped
1 small onion, chopped
½ pound ham steak, diced
3 eggs, slightly beaten
1 pound Monterey Jack cheese,
shredded
½ cup milk
¼ cup sour cream
½ teaspoon salt
¼ teaspoon cayenne pepper
¼ teaspoon pepper
1 10-inch unbaked pie shell

•

Preheat the oven to 375°F.

Place the bacon in a skillet and cook until browned. Remove the bacon from the skillet with a slotted spoon and drain on paper towels. Pour off most of the bacon drippings from the skillet. Add the onion and ham and sauté for 5 minutes.

Combine the bacon, onions and ham in a mixing bowl and toss. Add the eggs and cheese and mix again. Add the milk, sour cream, salt, cayenne and pepper and mix thoroughly.

Pour the mixture into the unbaked pie shell and bake for 30 minutes. Serve immediately.

PEACH 'N' PORK CHOP BARBECUE

serves 6

6 thick pork chops
1 tablespoon lemon juice
½ teaspoon salt
½ teaspoon black pepper
2 tablespoons butter
¼ cup firmly packed brown sugar
1 teaspoon cinnamon
½ teaspoon ground cloves
8 ounces tomato sauce
6 canned peach halves, reserving ¼ cup
syrup
¼ cup cider vinegar

•

Sprinkle the chops with the lemon juice and rub them with the salt and pepper. Melt the butter in a large skillet and brown the chops on both sides for 5 minutes.

Combine the brown sugar, cinnamon, cloves, tomato sauce, reserved peach syrup and vinegar in a bowl. Pour off most of the drippings in the skillet and top each chop with a peach half.

Pour the sauce over the chops and cover. Simmer over low heat for 30 minutes.

PORK CHOPS WITH POTATO SAUCE

serves 6

2 eggs
1 teaspoon paprika
1 clove garlic, minced
½ teaspoon salt
¼ teaspoon black pepper
1 teaspoon dry mustard
6 thick pork chops
1 cup cracker meal
vegetable oil for frying
½ cup chopped onion
1 small carrot, grated
2 tablespoons chopped pimento
3 tablespoons sifted flour
1⅓ cups water
½ cup light cream
½ teaspoon salt
¼ teaspoon black pepper
1 garlic clove, minced
2 cups mashed potatoes

•

Beat the eggs with the paprika, garlic, salt, pepper and mustard in a bowl. Blend well. Place the cracker meal in a second bowl.

Dip the chops in the egg mixture and dredge them in the cracker meal.

Fill a large heavy skillet with oil to a depth of ¼ inch. Heat over medium heat. When oil is very hot, add the pork chops and fry for 7 minutes on each side. Drain on paper towels and place in a slightly buttered casserole dish. Preheat the oven to 300°F.

Add the onion and carrot to the skillet with the oil and sauté for 5 minutes. Add the pimento and sauté for 2 minutes. Stir in the flour until well blended. Simmer for 2 minutes. Stir in the water, cream, salt, pepper and garlic and bring almost to a boil. Stir in the mashed potatoes and remove the skillet from the heat. Continue to stir until smooth.

Pour the sauce over the chops and bake, covered, for 15 minutes.

ORANGE PORK CHOPS

serves 4

4 thick center-cut pork chops
½ teaspoon salt
½ teaspoon black pepper
6 tablespoons flour
3 tablespoons butter
1 large orange, peeled and thinly sliced
½ cup orange juice
1 teaspoon cinnamon

•

Preheat the oven to 350°F. Rub the chops with the salt and pepper and dredge in the flour. Melt the butter in a skillet and brown the chops on both sides for 4 minutes.

Arrange the chops in one layer in a shallow baking dish. Cover each chop with 2 orange slices and add the orange juice. Sprinkle with cinnamon and bake, covered, for 45 minutes.

ROAST PORK

serves 8

1 4-pound center-cut pork loin
2 garlic cloves, minced
1 teaspoon salt
1 teaspoon black pepper
4 bay leaves
½ cup vinegar
½ teaspoon thyme
1 teaspoon chopped parsley

•

Preheat the oven to 325°F. With a small, sharp knife, pierce 8 slits into the top of the roast. Fill the slits with the minced garlic. Sprinkle with the salt and pepper.

Put the bay leaves on the bottom of a roasting pan and place the roast on top. Combine the vinegar, thyme and parsley in a bowl and pour over the roast. Roast for 2½ hours, basting every 15 minutes with the pan liquids.

ROAST PORK WITH TURNIPS

serves 4 to 6

1 3½-pound smoked pork shoulder
1½ pounds turnips, peeled and quartered
2 tablespoons cider vinegar
salt to taste
black pepper to taste

•

Preheat the oven to 325°F.

Tie the pork tightly with string and place it in a lightly oiled roasting pan. Roast for 1 hour.

After the pork has roasted for 50 minutes, begin to cook the turnips. Steam the turnips in a steamer or a little bit of water. Bring the water to a boil, then lower the heat and simmer, covered, for 8 to 10 minutes.

When the pork has roasted for 1 hour, add the turnips to the roasting pan and mix them with the pork drippings. Return the roast to the oven for 30 minutes.

Remove the pork to a cutting board. Pour the vinegar over the turnips in the roasting pan and mix well. Slice the pork and serve surrounded with turnips.

PORK SAUSAGE

serves 8

3 pounds ground lean pork
1 teaspoon dried sage
2 garlic cloves, finely minced
2 teaspoons salt
1 teaspoon pepper
1 tablespoon finely minced parsley
1 teaspoon cayenne pepper
sausage casing

•

In a large mixing bowl blend all the ingredients thoroughly with your hands.

Shape the mixture into patties or stuff the mixture into the casing, to a depth of 3 inches. Pinch the casing just above the stuffing and twist several times before stuffing again.

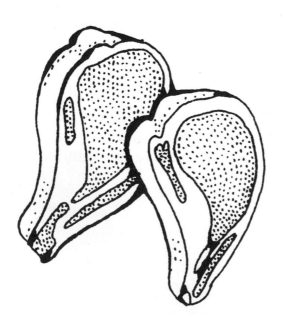

STEWED PORK WITH YAMS AND APPLES

serves 6

2 pounds lean stewing pork, cubed
4 tablespoons lemon juice
4 tablespoons butter
2 cups stewed tomatoes
¼ cup chopped parsley
1 teaspoon sugar
½ teaspoon salt
¼ teaspoon cayenne pepper
2 yams or sweet potatoes, very thinly sliced
4 apples, peeled, cored and sliced into wedges
2 tablespoons honey

•

Sprinkle the meat with 2 tablespoons lemon juice. Let stand 10 minutes.

Melt the butter in a large, heavy skillet. Add the pork and brown on all sides.

Stir in the stewed tomatoes, parsley, remaining lemon juice, sugar, salt and cayenne pepper. Simmer for 5 minutes. Stir in the yams and apples and bring to a boil. Stir in the honey, lower the heat and simmer for 15 minutes.

SMITHFIELD HAM

serves 12

1 12-pound Smithfield or other
high-quality ham
½ cup vinegar
1 cup firmly packed brown sugar
1 cup apple cider
2 bay leaves
20 whole cloves
1 large can sliced pineapple, with syrup
reserved
1 bottle maraschino cherries, drained

●

Put the ham in a large roasting pan and cover with cold water. Soak for 2 hours. Drain the ham. Rub the surface with a stiff brush under cold running water. Return the ham to the roasting pan, cover with cold water again, and soak for 24 hours. Change the water twice during the 24 hours.

Drain the ham again and cover with cold water. Add the vinegar, ½ cup brown sugar, cider and bay leaves. Stir well. Place the roasting pan over two burners on the stove. Bring to a boil and lower the heat. Simmer, uncovered, for 4 hours.

Preheat the oven to 375°F. Remove the ham from the roasting pan and allow to cool slightly. Slice off the fat from the surface leaving a half-inch layer. Drain the water from the roasting pan. Put the ham back in the pan and stud the surface with the cloves. Makes a paste of the remaining brown sugar and pineapple syrup in a bowl. Brush the ham with the paste and arrange the pineapple rings over the top. Place the cherries in the centers of the rings. Bake, uncovered, for 30 minutes.

QUICK GLAZED HAM

serves 10

1 10-pound ham, with bone
20 whole cloves
1 cup French-style mustard
2 cups firmly packed brown sugar
2 tablespoons chopped parsley

●

Preheat the oven to 325°F. Trim off excess fat and rind from the ham. Score the top of the ham into large diamond-shaped cuts 1-inch deep. Place the ham in a roasting pan. Insert a clove into the center of each diamond.

Combine the mustard and brown sugar in a bowl and blend well. Brush the entire ham with the glaze. Pour any remaining glaze over the top of the ham. Sprinkle the ham with the parsley.

Use aluminum foil to form an enclosed tent over the ham, being careful not to let the foil rest on the ham. Bake for 3½ hours.

STUFFED PORK CHOPS

serves 6

6 thick pork chops
4 tablespoons lemon juice
6 tablespoons cream cheese, softened
1 tablespoon chopped parsley
1 garlic clove, finely minced
1 scallion, finely chopped
½ teaspoon paprika
¼ teaspoon cinnamon
3 tablespoons butter
1 teaspoon oregano

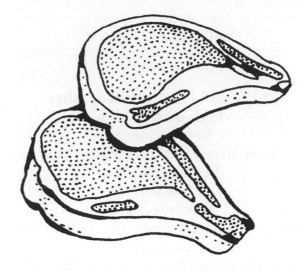

●

Sprinkle 2 tablespoons lemon juice on both sides of the chops. Rub the juice into the meat. Slice deep pockets in the sides of the chops.

In a bowl, combine the cream cheese, parsley, garlic, scallions, paprika and cinnamon and blend well. Stuff each chop with an equal portion of the mixture and secure the chops with toothpicks.

Place the butter in pats in a large skillet. Sprinkle with 1 tablespoon lemon juice. Sprinkle half the oregano over the butter and add the chops.

Set the skillet over medium heat cook for 8 minutes. Sprinkle with remaining lemon juice and orega Turn the chops carefully and cool the second side for 8 minutes. Se immediately.

STEWS AND GUMBOS

BRUNSWICK STEW

serves 8

2 3-pounds chickens, cut into serving
pieces
2 pounds boneless veal shoulder,
in 1 piece
1 ham bone
3 quarts water
½ cup sugar
1 bay leaf
1 teaspoon dried basil
1 tablespoon chopped parsley
2 onions, sliced
4 cups tomatoes, peeled and chopped
4 celery sticks with leaves, chopped
2 cups fresh lima beans
4 cups corn kernels
½ cup butter
1 teaspoon hot red pepper flakes
4 medium-sized potatoes, peeled,
cooked and mashed

•

In a large pot combine the chicken, veal, ham bone, water, sugar, bay leaf, basil and parsley. Cook over low heat until the veal and chicken are very tender, about 50 minutes.

Remove the veal and chicken pieces from the broth and set aside.

Add the onions, tomatoes, celery and lima beans to the broth. Cook over low heat until the beans are tender, about 15 minutes. Stir often.

Cut the veal into small pieces. Remove the chicken from the bones and cut into small pieces. Discard the bones and skin.

Return the veal and chicken meat to the pot. Add the corn and simmer the stew for 10 minutes.

Stir in the butter, red pepper flakes and pepper. Season to taste with salt.

Stir the mashed potatoes into the stew. Cook, stirring constantly, for 15 minutes or until the stew thickens and the potatoes are absorbed. Serve hot.

CHICKEN AND OKRA GUMBO

serves 6

1 2½-pound chicken, skinned, boned
and chunked
5 tablespoons butter
3 tablespoons flour
1 tablespoon chopped parsley
1 onion, chopped
1 pound fresh okra, trimmed and
halved
1 teaspoon salt
1 teaspoon cayenne pepper
2 cups water
2 cups chicken broth

•

Lightly brown the chicken in the butter, in a large pot. Stir in the flour and continue to brown. Stir in the parsley and onions and continue browning.

Stir in the okra and continue cooking, stirring constantly. Stir in the salt, cayenne pepper, water and broth and bring to a boil. Lower the heat and simmer for 1 hour.

CHICKEN JAMBALAYA

serves 10

5 tablespoons bacon drippings
3 pounds boneless and skinless
chicken, in large chunks
2 onions, chopped
2 red bell peppers, chopped
2 garlic cloves, minced
2 tablespoons flour
½ pound lean baked ham, cubed
1½ pounds lean pork, cubed
6 smoked hot sausages, thinly sliced
1 pound cooked shrimp, shelled and
deveined
1 teaspoon salt
1 teaspoon black pepper
1 teaspoon hot red-pepper sauce
2 bay leaves
1½ cups long-grained rice
2 cups hot chicken broth
1 cup hot white wine

•

Heat the bacon drippings in a large heavy pot and stir in the chicken. Brown the chicken pieces quickly on all sides, stirring constantly.

Remove the chicken and drain on paper towels. Add the onions, red bell pepper and garlic to the pot and sauté for 5 minutes. Sprinkle in the flour and blend well.

Add the ham and pork and simmer, stirring constantly, for 2 minutes. Add the sausages, stir well and cook over medium heat for 3 minutes. Add the shrimp, salt, pepper, hot red-pepper sauce, bay leaves, rice, broth, reserved chicken and wine. Bring to a boil.

Reduce heat and simmer, covered, for 25 minutes. Uncover and cook for 5 minutes more.

CREOLE JAMBALAYA

serves 8

1 tablespoon butter
1 pound smoked pork sausage, cubed
1 green bell pepper, chopped
1 tablespoon flour
3 cups cooked whole shrimp, shelled
and deveined
3 tomatoes, peeled and diced
2½ cups water
1 onion, coarsely chopped
1 garlic clove, minced
2 tablespoons chopped parsley
2 cups raw long-grained rice
2 tablespoons Worcestershire sauce
1½ teaspoons salt
½ teaspoon oregano
½ teaspoon hot red pepper flakes

•

Melt the butter in a skillet and add the sauce. Brown the sausage well. Add the green bell pepper and simmer, stirring, for 5 minutes. Add the flour and blend well. Simmer for 2 minutes more.

Add the shrimp and tomatoes and simmer for 2 minutes, stirring constantly. Stir in the water, onion, garlic and parsley and bring to a boil. Lower the heat, stir in the rice, Worcestershire sauce, salt, oregano and red pepper. Cover and simmer for 30 minutes or until the water is absorbed.

CRAB STEW

serves 4

3 pounds crab legs
2 tablespoons butter
1 small onion, chopped
2 cups thinly sliced mushrooms
2 tomatoes, peeled and chopped
¼ teaspoon cayenne pepper
1 cup heavy cream
½ cup light cream
½ teaspoon salt
2 tablespoons chopped parsley
1 teaspoon chopped chives
¼ cup brandy

•

In a large pot, bring 3 quarts of water to a boil over high heat. Add the crab legs. When the water returns to a boil, reduce the heat to low and simmer the crab legs for 10 minutes.

While the crab legs are cooking, melt the butter in a large skillet. Add the onion and cook, stirring constantly, over medium heat for 2 minutes. Add the mushrooms and continue to cook, stirring frequently, for 2 minutes more. Add the tomatoes and cook, stirring frequently, for 5 minutes more. Reduce the heat to low and let the mixture simmer gently.

Drain the crab legs. Shell the crabmeat and remove the cartilage. Break the crabmeat into small pieces and add to the skillet. Increase the heat to medium.

Stir in the cayenne pepper, heavy cream, light cream and salt to taste. Continue to stir until the mixture comes to a boil.

Remove the skillet from the heat and stir in the parsley, chives and brandy. Serve the stew hot over rice.

CRAB CASSEROLE

serves 6

½ cup unflavored breadcrumbs
3 tablespoons melted butter
2 cups flaked crabmeat
1 cup soft unflavored breadcrumbs
¼ cup light cream
1½ cups mayonnaise
6 hard-cooked eggs, diced
1 tablespoon minced parsley
½ teaspoon salt
¼ teaspoon black pepper
¼ teaspoon hot red pepper flakes

•

Preheat the oven to 325°F. Mix the ½ cup breadcrumbs with the butter in a bowl and set aside.

Combine the crabmeat, soft breadcrumbs, light cream, mayonnaise, eggs, parsley, salt, pepper and red pepper in a bowl. Turn the mixture into a buttered casserole dish and sprinkle the buttered breadcrumbs over the top. Bake 25 minutes. Serve hot.

CRAWFISH CREOLE

serves 6

2 bay leaves
¼ teaspoon whole cloves
12 black peppercorns
1 parsley sprig
1 cinnamon stick
2 cups milk
2 tablespoons butter
2 tablespoons flour
1 teaspoon cayenne pepper
1 teaspoon hot red-pepper sauce
1 teaspoon nutmeg
½ teaspoon salt
3 tomatoes, seeded and finely chopped
36 crawfish, shelled and diced
12 mushrooms, finely chopped

•

Put the bay leaves, cloves, peppercorns, parsley and cinnamon stick on a square of cheesecloth. Tie the square closed to make an herb bouquet. Set aside.

In a medium-sized saucepan, bring the milk to a boil over medium heat. While the milk heats, melt the butter in a large saucepan. Add the flour and cook, stirring often, for 3 minutes. When the milk boils, gradually stir it into the butter mixture. Stir in the cayenne pepper, hot red-pepper sauce, nutmeg and salt. Add the herb bouquet and cook over medium heat for 15 minutes.

Remove the herb bouquet and add the tomatoes, crawfish meat and mushrooms. Cook over medium heat for 5 minutes, stirring often. Serve hot.

HEARTY BEEF STEW

serves 8

3 tablespoons butter
1 onion, chopped
2 pounds extra lean beef, cubed
2 tablespoons flour
1 cup beef broth
1 teaspoon salt
½ teaspoon black pepper
½ teaspoon savory
½ teaspoon oregano
1 teaspoon Worcestershire sauce
3 tablespoons lemon juice
1 tablespoon chopped parsley
3 tomatoes, chopped
3 zucchini, sliced
3 carrots, julienned
4 celery stalks, coarsely chopped
½ cup white wine

•

Melt the butter in a large saucepan and sauté the onion. Stir in the beef and brown thoroughly on all sides. Sprinkle in the flour and stir until well blended.

Stir in the beef broth and simmer for 5 minutes. Stir in the salt, pepper, savory, oregano, Worcestershire sauce, lemon juice, parsley, tomatoes, zucchini, carrots, celery and wine and bring to a boil.

Lower the heat and simmer for 30 minutes. Serve over rice.

CURRIED SHELLFISH WITH SPINACH

serves 6

12 large shrimp
12 sea scallops
12 crab legs
1 large lobster tail
8 tablespoons butter
1 small onion, chopped
1 red bell pepper, sliced into rings
1 green bell pepper, sliced into rings
4 garlic cloves, finely chopped
12 small white mushrooms
2 scallions, chopped
4 teaspoons curry powder
½ teaspoon cayenne pepper
½ teaspoon hot red-pepper sauce
salt to taste
2 cups dry white wine
½ pound fresh spinach, rinsed well

•

Put the shrimp, scallops, crab legs and lobster tail into a steamer basket. Steam the seafood over boiling water for 5 minutes. Remove the seafood from the steamer and let cool. Shell and devein the shrimp. Shell the crab legs and break the meat into chunks. Shell the lobster tail and cut the meat into chunks. Set the seafood aside.

Melt the butter in a large skillet. Add the onions, red bell pepper, green bell pepper and garlic. Cook over low heat, stirring constantly, until the vegetables are tender. Add the mushrooms, scallions, curry powder, cayenne pepper, hot red-pepper sauce and salt to taste. Stir well. Add the reserved shellfish and stir again. Cook over low heat, stirring constantly, for 5 minutes.

Add the wine to the skillet and bring the liquid to a boil over medium heat. Remove the skillet from the heat and add the spinach leaves. Stir gently for 3 minutes, or until the spinach is wilted and bright green. Transfer the curry to a serving bowl and serve hot.

GUMBO FILÉ

serves 6

1 5-pound chicken, cut into serving
pieces
2 teaspoons salt
1 teaspoon black pepper
1 garlic clove, chopped
3 tablespoons butter
2 medium-sized onions, chopped
½ pound boiled ham, cut into strips
3 quarts water
½ teaspoon dried thyme
½ teaspoon dried rosemary
¼ teaspoon chili powder
1 cup canned tomatoes
1 cup sliced fresh okra
24 oysters, shelled
1 tablespoon filé powder

•

Rub the salt, pepper and garlic pieces
into the chicken.

In a large saucepan, melt the butter.
Add the onions and the chicken and
cook until the chicken pieces are
lightly browned, about 8 minutes.
Add the ham, water, thyme, rosemary, chili powder and tomatoes.
Cover and simmer for 2½ hours.

Add the okra and cook 1 hour longer.

Add the oysters. Bring the mixture
to a boil and cook for 3 minutes.

Remove the saucepan from the heat
and stir in filé powder. Mix well. Do
not allow the gumbo to boil. Do not
reheat the gumbo after the filé
powder has been added or the
gumbo will become stringy. Serve
hot in soup bowls.

JUBAL'S GUMBO

serves 10

1 2- to 3-pound frying chicken, cut into
stew-sized pieces
2 tablespoons butter
1 pound smoked pork sausage, sweet
or hot, sliced
¼ cup vegetable oil
4 tablespoons flour
1 green pepper, chopped
1 red pepper, chopped
¼ cup chopped parsley
1 cup chopped celery
1 garlic clove, minced
3 tablespoons Worcestershire sauce
¼ teaspoon Tabasco sauce
½ cup chopped scallion

•

Melt the butter in a large stew pot.
Add the chicken pieces and sausage
slices and lightly brown. Remove the
chicken and sausage and set aside.

Add the vegetable oil to the drippings in the skillet and heat for
1 minute. Slowly stir in the flour,
stirring constantly to avoid lumps.
Reduce the heat to low and continue
to cook until the mixture becomes a
rich brown gravy.

Return the chicken and sausage to
the skillet. Add the green pepper,
red pepper, parsley, celery, garlic,
Worcestershire sauce and Tabasco
sauce. Cover the skillet and simmer
over low heat for 1 hour, or until all
the ingredients are tender.

Sprinkle the chopped scallion over
the gumbo and serve over hot rice.

JUNGLE STEW

serves 8

4 tablespoons olive oil
2 onions, chopped
1 green bell pepper, chopped
1 red bell pepper, chopped
2 cloves garlic, minced
2 pounds lean beef stew meat, cubed
1 cup elbow macaroni
2 15-ounce cans red beans, (reserving
the liquid from one)
2 1-pound cans stewed tomatoes
1 teaspoon salt
1 teaspoon black pepper
½ teaspoon cayenne pepper
½ teaspoon sugar

•

Heat the olive oil in a large skillet. Add the onions, green bell pepper, red bell pepper and garlic and sauté for 5 minutes, stirring constantly.

Add the stew meat and cook until browned. Add the macaroni, red beans, reserved liquid, stewed tomatoes, salt, pepper, cayenne pepper and sugar.

Blend well and simmer over medium heat until the macaroni is tender, about 25 minutes. Serve hot.

KENTUCKY BURGOO

serves 10

5 tablespoons butter or olive oil
1 pound lean beef, cubed
½ pound lean veal, cubed
3 pounds boneless and skinless
chicked, cubed
2 onions, chopped
2 garlic cloves, minced
2 potatoes, peeled and diced
4 celery stalks, chopped
3 carrots, julienned
1 green bell pepper, chopped
2 quarts water
1 tablespoon salt
1 pound beef round bones, with
marrow
2 cups stewed tomatoes
1 onion, cut into wedges
1 cup fresh butter beans
½ teaspoon hot red pepper flakes
1 bay leaf
¼ cup brown sugar
1 teaspoon black pepper
½ teaspoon cayenne pepper
1 cup sliced fresh okra
2 cups corn kernels
¼ cup butter
½ cup flour, sifted

•

Melt the butter in a deep heavy pot and stir in the beef, veal and chicken. Quickly brown the meat on all sides.

Stir in the onions, garlic, potatoes, celery, carrots and green bell pepper and cook for 3 minutes, stirring constantly. Add the water, salt, beef bones, tomatoes, onion wedges, butter beans, red pepper flakes, bay leaf, sugar, black pepper, and cayenne pepper and stir well. Bring to a boil and lower the heat. Simmer for 2 hours, covered.

Add the okra and corn and stir thoroughly. Melt the butter in a small saucepan and add the flour. Blend well and mix into the pot. Stir thoroughly and simmer for 15 minutes more.

LAMB STEW

serves 6

3 tablespoons olive oil
2 pounds lean lamb shoulder, cubed
1 onion, chopped
½ teaspoon salt
½ teaspoon basil
½ teaspoon oregano
½ teaspoon chopped fresh mint
3 tomatoes, chopped
8 ounces tomato sauce
2 garlic cloves, finely minced
1 teaspoon sugar
1 small green bell pepper, julienned

•

Heat the oil in a large skillet and brown the meat. Add the onions and sauté for 4 minutes.

Add the salt, basil, oregano, mint, tomatoes, tomato sauce, garlic and sugar and simmer over medium heat for 15 minutes. Add the green bell pepper and simmer for 10 minutes longer. Serve hot over rice.

OLD CREOLE VEGETABLE GUMBO

serves 6

2 tablespoons olive oil
1 large eggplant, peeled and cubed
2 green peppers, seeded and cut into
1-inch pieces
2 carrots, peeled and sliced
2 small new potatoes, quartered
½ pound okra, halved
1 red onion, peeled and chopped
2 garlic cloves, sliced
2 cups stewed whole tomatoes
½ teaspoon sugar
1 teaspoon salt
½ teaspoon hot red pepper flakes
¼ teaspoon grated nutmeg

•

Heat the olive oil in a large saucepan and add all the ingredients. Cover the saucepan and simmer over low heat for about 1½ hours, stirring every 15 minutes.

Serve hot over rice or thin egg noodles.

OYSTER STEW WITH SESAME SEEDS

serves 8

4 tablespoons sesame seeds
2 onions, thinly sliced
6 strips bacon or salt pork
3 tablespoons flour
2 cups oyster liquor or 1 cup water and
1 cup dry sherry
3 cups shelled oysters

•

Preheat the oven to 450°F.

Spread the sesame seeds (also called benne seeds) on a foil-covered baking sheet. Toast the seeds in the oven until they are browned. Set aside.

Fry the bacon and onion in a heavy stew pot until the bacon is cooked but not crisp. Remove the bacon and onion and set aside. Leave the drippings in the pot.

Reduce the heat a little and slowly stir in the flour, continuing to stir until the drippings become a rich brown gravy. Gradually stir in the oyster liquor until it is thoroughly blended. Simmer the mixture over medium heat, stirring constantly for about 5 minutes, or until the mixture has thickened and is very smooth.

Put the reserved sesame seeds into a small plastic bag. Seal the bag and crush the seeds with a rolling pin until they are a coarse powder. Add the powder to the stew and stir well.

Chop the reserved bacon strips into small pieces, and add them and the reserved onion to the stew. Add the oysters and cook them 5 to 10 minutes, or until the edges of the oysters curl.

Serve piping hot over hominy.

PINE BARK STEW

serves 10

½ pound bacon, coarsely chopped
5 large potatoes, peeled and diced
4 cups stewed tomatoes
3 onions, cut into wedges
2 quarts water
3 pounds skinned catfish fillets, cut into pieces
1 cup tomato sauce
½ teaspoon salt
½ teaspoon black pepper

•

Cook the bacon in a large pot until it is lightly browned.

Stir in the potatoes, tomatoes and onions and simmer for 5 minutes. Add the water, cover and simmer over low heat for 2 hours.

Add the catfish, tomato sauce, salt and pepper and simmer for 20 minutes more.

VEAL STEW CREOLE

serves 6

4 pounds veal brisket
½ pound ham, diced
2 large onions, chopped
2 sweet potatoes, peeled and cubed
2 dozen small fresh okra, very thinly
sliced
6 medium-sized tomatoes, chopped
2 garlic cloves, finely chopped
2 tablespoons butter
1 bay leaf
2 parsley sprigs
½ teaspoon dried thyme
salt to taste
black pepper to taste
cayenne pepper to taste

•

Cut the veal into pieces about 3 inches long and 2 inches wide. Season the pieces with salt, pepper and cayenne pepper.

Melt 1 tablespoon of the butter in a large heavy pot. Brown the veal in the butter, approximately 3 to 5 minutes per side. Add the ham and sweet potatoes and simmer gently for 15 minutes.

Meanwhile, prepare the sauce. In a saucepan melt the remaining butter. Add the onions and brown. Add the bay leaf, parsley and thyme. Add the tomatoes and cook for 15 minutes.

Add the sauce to the veal. Mix thoroughly, cover tightly and simmer over low heat for 2 hours.

Add the okra, simmer 30 minutes longer and serve.

PLANTATION CHICKEN AND VEGETABLE STEW

serves 6

1 4-pound roasting chicken, cut into
stew-sized pieces
3 tablespoons vegetable oil
1½ cups water
½ cup sherry
1 tablespoon salt
½ teaspoon white pepper
10 white onions, halved
1 cup fresh green peas
1 cup sliced peeled carrots
½ cup diced peeled turnip
1 cup diced peeled potatoes
½ cup corn
⅓ cup flour
½ cup warm water
chopped parsley

•

Heat the vegetable oil in a Dutch oven or large heavy pot. Add the chicken pieces and brown them on all sides. Add the water, sherry, salt and pepper. Cover and simmer over medium heat for 45 minutes.

Add the onions, green peas, carrots, turnip, potatoes and corn to the stew. Cover and simmer for another 40 minutes.

Combine the flour and warm water in a bowl. Stir the mixture into the stew. Continue to cook for another 5 to 8 minutes, or until the stew thickens. Serve over rice.

SHRIMP GUMBO

serves 6

8 tablespoons butter
2 garlic cloves, finely minced
2 small green bell peppers, coarsely
chopped
2 small red bell peppers, coarsely
chopped
2 medium-sized onions, finely chopped
3 cups whole canned tomatoes
1 bay leaf
¼ teaspoon cayenne pepper
½ teaspoon hot red-pepper sauce
salt to taste
black pepper to taste
2 pounds medium-sized shrimp,
shelled and deveined

•

In a large saucepan melt the butter over low heat. Add the garlic, red bell peppers and green bell peppers and mix well. Add the onions. Cook, stirring constantly, for 2 minutes. Add the tomatoes, bay leaf, cayenne pepper, hot red-pepper sauce and salt and pepper to taste. Stir gently but thoroughly. Half cover the saucepan and simmer for 25 minutes.

Add the shrimp to the mixture in the saucepan and cook for 5 minutes. Serve immediately with rice.

VEGETABLE STEW

serves an army

5 quarts water
3 cups white wine
1 cup lemon juice
3 tablespoons salt
1 tablespoon black pepper
1 tablespoon oregano
5 bay leaves
5 cloves
2 cinnamon sticks
1 tablespoon sugar
8 carrots, sliced
8 celery stalks, coarsely chopped
8 potatoes, cut into wedges
4 zucchini, sliced
4 yellow squash, sliced
1 pound mushrooms, quartered
8 tomatoes, chopped
4 onions, cut into wedges
1 pound green beans, trimmed and
halved
3 cups corn kernels

•

In a 10-quart pot combine the water, wine, lemon juice, 2 tablespoons salt, pepper, oregano, sugar, bay leaves, cloves and cinnamon stick. Bring to a boil and simmer over low heat for 1 hour.

Add the carrots, celery, potatoes, zucchini and yellow squash and simmer for 30 minutes.

Add the mushrooms, tomatoes, onions, green beans, corn and 1 tablespoon salt and bring back to a boil. Lower heat and simmer for 30 minutes.

WET HASH

serves 4

3 tablespoons butter
1 large onion, chopped
1 celery stalk, finely chopped
3 unpeeled large potatoes, diced
2 tablespoons flour
2 cups shredded cooked beef
1 cup beef bouillon
½ teaspoon salt
½ teaspoon cayenne pepper
1 teaspoon Worcestershire sauce

●

Melt the butter in a large skillet and sauté the onion and celery for 5 minutes. Add the potatoes and flour, stir well and continue to cook for 5 minutes. Add the beef and cook for 5 minutes. Add the bouillon, salt, cayenne pepper and Worcestershire sauce. Blend well and simmer over low heat for 15 minutes. Serve over rice.

BREADS

BATTER BREAD

serves 6

3 eggs
1 cup milk
1 cup buttermilk
⅓ cup white cornmeal
2 teaspoons baking powder
¼ teaspoon baking soda
½ teaspoon salt
2 tablespoons melted butter

•

Preheat the oven to 400°F. Grease an 8-inch square baking pan.

Beat together in a bowl the eggs, milk and buttermilk. Beat well. Sift together the cornmeal, baking powder, soda and salt in another bowl. Pour the egg and milk mixture over the dry ingredients and blend thoroughly. Blend in the butter. Turn the dough into the prepared baking pan and bake for 1 hour.

BREAKFAST BREAD

makes 1 loaf

1 cup warm water
1 package active dried yeast
½ cup honey
1 teaspoon salt
2½ cups flour
1 egg
½ cup corn oil
2 teaspoons grated lemon rind
½ cup chopped walnuts
½ cup white currants
½ cup raspberry preserves or drained canned raspberries

•

Put the warm water in a mixing bowl and dissolve the yeast in it. Stir in the honey, salt and 1½ cups of the flour. Beat with electric mixer until smooth, about 2 minutes. Beat in the egg, corn oil, lemon rind, walnuts and currants. Mix thoroughly until well blended.

Turn the dough out onto a lightly floured surface. With your hands, pound the dough into a flat oblong about 8 inches wide. Spread the raspberry preserves or canned raspberries on top of the flattened dough. Roll up the dough into a loaf shape and place it in a buttered 1½-quart baking dish. Cover the loaf with a towel and let it rise in a warm place until it is doubled in size.

Preheat the oven to 375°F. Bake the bread for 30 minutes, brushing with beaten egg white every 10 minutes for a shiny, crisp crust.

BENNE BISCUITS

serves 6

2 cups flour
1 teaspoon salt
⅛ teaspoon cayenne pepper
¾ cup butter
¼ cup ice water
1 cup sesame seeds
salt

•

Preheat the oven to 350°F.

In a large bowl mix the flour, 1 teaspoon salt and cayenne pepper. With a pastry blender or two knives, cut in the butter. Add enough ice water to make a dough with the consistency of pie crust.

Spread the sesame seeds in a shallow baking dish. Roast them in the oven for 20 minutes, or until the seeds are well browned. Shake the pan during roasting to turn the seeds. Remove the sesame seeds and lower the oven temperature to 300°F.

Add the sesame seeds to the dough mixture and stir well. On a lightly floured surface, roll the dough out to ¼-inch thickness. Cut circles from the dough with a small round biscuit cutter. Place the rounds in muffin pans and bake them for 20 to 30 minutes, or until browned. Before removing the biscuits from the pans, sprinkle them with salt. Cool completely.

Store the benne biscuits in tins. To crisp, heat them in a 300°F oven before serving.

BUCKWHEAT CAKES

serves 2

½ cup sifted buckwheat flour
½ cup sifted whole wheat flour
2 teaspoons baking powder
¼ teaspoon salt
1 egg
¾ cup milk
1½ teaspoons molasses

•

Sift together the buckwheat flour and the whole wheat flour with the baking powder and salt in a bowl. In another bowl blend together the egg, milk and molasses and pour over the dry ingredients. Blend well and spoon onto a lightly greased griddle. Cook until bubbly and firm around the edges; flip and cook the other side. Serve with butter and molasses or maple syrup.

Glazed Carrots

Cornbread

Trout with Almonds and Pine Nuts

BUTTERMILK BISCUITS

makes 2 dozen

2 cups flour, sifted
2½ teaspoons baking powder
1 teaspoon salt
¼ teaspoon baking soda
⅓ cup solid white shortening
¾ cup buttermilk
¼ cup light cream

•

Preheat the oven to 450°F.

Sift together in a bowl the flour, baking powder, salt and soda; cut in the shortening with a pastry blender. Stir in the buttermilk and mix lightly Gently form the dough into a ball and place on a floured surface. Knead the dough gently for 3 minutes. Roll the dough out to a thickness of one-half inch. Cut out 24 round biscuits with a floured pastry cutter or floured knife. Place close together on an ungreased baking sheet and bake for 12 minutes.

BUTTERMILK CORNCAKES

serves 4

2 eggs, slightly beaten
1 cup buttermilk
1 cup water
1 cup white cornmeal
1 cup flour
½ teaspoon baking soda
½ teaspoon salt
bacon drippings or vegetable oil

•

Mix together the eggs, buttermilk and water in a bowl. In another bowl blend the cornmeal, flour, soda and salt together. Combine the two mixtures and blend well.

Fill a large heavy skillet with bacon drippings or vegetable oil to a depth of one-quarter inch. Place over medium heat.

Drop the batter by the heaping tablespoonful into the skillet. Cook until bubbles form; flip and cook until lightly browned.

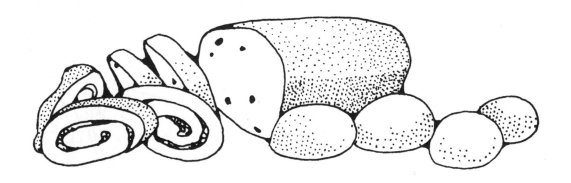

CHEESE BISCUITS

serves 6

¼ pound softened butter
2 egg yolks, beaten
¾ cup grated Swiss cheese
½ tablespoon French-style mustard
¼ teaspoon cayenne pepper
1 cup sifted flour

●

Preheat the oven to 300°F. Beat the butter in a large bowl until smooth and creamy. Add the egg yolks and mix well. Blend in the cheese, mustard and cayenne pepper. Gradually stir in the flour and mix well. Form the dough into a ball and transfer to a floured cutting board. Roll the dough out to a thickness of one-half inch. Cut into 12 round biscuits with a floured pastry cutter or floured knife. Place on a lightly buttered baking sheet and bake for 20 minutes.

CORNSTICKS

serves 4

1½ cups yellow cornmeal
½ cup flour, sifted
1 teaspoon baking powder
1 teaspoon baking soda
2 teaspoons sugar
2 eggs, beaten
2 cups buttermilk
3 tablespoons melted butter

●

Preheat the oven to 425°F. Sift together the cornmeal, flour, baking powder, soda and sugar in a bowl. Beat together the eggs, buttermilk and butter in another bowl. Blend the two mixtures together. Pour the mixture into a greased 12-stick cornstick pan and bake for 25 minutes.

CREOLE HONEY BREAD

makes 1 loaf

2 cups flour
1 teaspoon baking soda
1 teaspoon baking powder
1 teaspoon salt
1 teaspoon ground ginger
½ teaspoon cinnamon
1 cup milk
1 cup honey
1 egg, slightly beaten

●

Preheat the oven to 375°F.

Into a large bowl sift the flour, baking soda, baking powder, salt, ginger and cinnamon. Stir in the milk, honey and egg. Place in the bowl of an electric mixer and beat for 20 minutes or until all ingredients are well blended and the batter is smooth.

Pour the batter into a buttered 9 × 5 × 3-inch loaf pan. Bake for 45 minutes or until a cake tester inserted in the middle comes out clean.

Remove the bread from the oven and cool in the pan for 10 minutes. Turn the loaf out onto a rack and continue cooling. Serve the bread sliced thin.

CORNBREAD

serves 12

1 cup yellow cornmeal
1 cup sifted flour
1½ tablespoons sugar
2½ teaspoons baking powder
½ teaspoon baking soda
½ teaspoon salt
2 eggs, beaten
1½ cups buttermilk
¼ cup melted butter

●

Preheat the oven to 425°F. Sift together the cornmeal, flour, sugar, baking powder, soda and salt in a bowl. Beat the eggs and buttermilk together in another bowl and blend in the melted butter. Pour the egg mixture over the dry ingredients and blend thoroughly. Turn the mixture into a lightly buttered 8-inch square pan and bake for 25 minutes. Cut into squares and serve.

CREOLE FRENCH TOAST

serves 4

5 eggs, well beaten
½ cup milk
¼ cup sugar
½ teaspoon grated lemon rind
½ teaspoon salt
6 thick bread slices, trimmed and cut
into thick strips
1 cup unflavored breadcrumbs
lard or vegetable oil
confectioners' sugar

•

Beat the eggs well in a large bowl and beat in the milk, sugar, lemon rind and salt. Dip the bread strips in the batter and then in the bread-crumbs.

Fill a large heavy skillet with lard or vegetable oil to a depth of one-quarter inch. Place over medium heat. Add the bread strips to the hot oil and fry until golden brown. Dust with the confectioners' sugar and serve.

DOUGHNUTS

makes 2 dozen

1 cup sugar
3½ teaspoons baking powder
½ teaspoon cinnamon
½ teaspoon nutmeg
½ teaspoon salt
4 cups sifted flour
2 eggs
1 cup milk
3 tablespoons melted butter
oil for frying

•

Sift together the sugar, baking powder, cinnamon, nutmeg, salt and flour in a large bowl. Beat the eggs with the milk in another bowl and stir into the flour mixture. Blend in the butter. Form a ball of dough and place on a floured cutting board. Shape the dough into a cylinder with a diameter of about 1 inch. Cut the cylinder into half-inch slices. Poke a hole in the center of each slice with your finger and form the slice into a doughnut shape.

Fill a large heavy skillet with oil to a depth of 1 inch. Heat until the oil is very hot, 375°F. Add the doughnuts, in batches if necessary, and fry until golden. Drain on paper towels. Dust with confectioners' sugar and serve immediately.

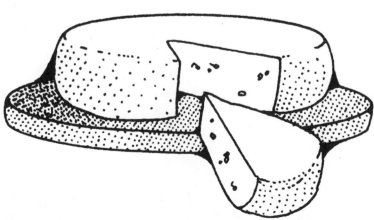

HOECAKE

serves 4

2 cups yellow cornmeal
1 teaspoon salt
1 cup light cream

•

Sift together the cornmeal and salt in a bowl. Blend with the light cream.

Pour heaping tablespoons of the batter onto a greased griddle over medium-low heat. Cook for 15 minutes or until covered with bubbles. Flip and cook the other side for 10 minutes.

HOMINY BREAD

serves 8

½ cup hominy grits
3 cups water
½ teaspoon salt
2 tablespoons butter
2 eggs, beaten
2 cups milk
1 cup white cornmeal

•

Combine the grits, water and salt in a saucepan and bring to a boil. Cover, reduce heat to low and simmer for 45 minutes.

Preheat the oven to 425°F. Remove the grits from the stove and stir in the butter, eggs and 1 cup of the milk. Blend in the cornmeal and remaining cup milk and pour into a greased baking dish. Bake for 45 minutes.

DROP BISCUITS

makes 1 dozen

2 cups flour
2 teaspoons baking powder
1 teaspoon salt
4 tablespoons butter
1 cup milk

•

Preheat the oven to 450°F.

Combine the flour with the baking powder and salt in a large bowl. Cut in the butter with a pastry blender or two knives until the mixture resembles a coarse meal. Add the milk and stir to form a soft dough.

Drop the dough by well-rounded tablespoons onto a lightly buttered baking sheet. There should be 12 biscuits.

Bake for 12 to 15 minutes or until golden. Serve hot.

GINGERBREAD WAFFLES

serves 6

2 eggs
¼ cup sugar
½ cup molasses
1 cup sour cream
1½ cups flour, sifted
1 teaspoon powdered ginger
¼ teaspoon ground cloves
¼ teaspoon cinnamon
¼ teaspoon salt
1 teaspoon baking soda
1 teaspoon baking powder
⅓ cup melted butter

•

Beat the eggs in a bowl and blend in the sugar, molasses and sour cream.

In another bowl combine the flour, ginger, cloves, cinnamon, salt, baking soda and baking powder. Blend thoroughly and pour in the melted butter. Mix well and bake on a waffle iron.

HUCKLEBERRY BREAD

makes 1 loaf

2 eggs
1 cup sugar
3 tablespoons melted butter
1 cup milk
3 cups flour
1 teaspoon salt
4 teaspoons baking powder
1 cup fresh huckleberries
½ cup chopped walnuts

•

Preheat the oven to 350°F.

In a large bowl beat the eggs. Gradually add the sugar and continue beating for 1 minute. Add the butter and milk. Stir until well blended.

In a bowl combine the huckleberries and the chopped nuts.

Combine the flour with salt and baking powder. Add to the huckleberries and nuts and stir gently. Add the mixture to the egg and milk mixture. Stir only until the dry ingredients are moistened.

Turn the dough into a buttered 5 × 12-inch loaf pan. Bake for 50 to 60 minutes or until a cake tester inserted into the center comes out clean.

Remove to a cooling rack and cool in the pan for 10 minutes. Turn out onto the rack and cool completely.

HUSH PUPPIES

serves 6

1½ cups yellow cornmeal
½ cup sifted flour
2 teaspoons baking powder
1 egg, well beaten
¾ cup milk
1 small onion, grated
1 teaspoon salt
½ teaspoon cayenne pepper
lard or vegetable oil for deep frying

•

Combine the cornmeal, flour and baking powder in a mixing bowl and set aside. Combine the beaten egg, milk, onion, salt and pepper in another bowl and set aside.

Fill a deep skillet to a depth of 1 inch with vegetable oil or lard and place over medium heat. Combine the cornmeal mixture with the liquid mixture and blend thoroughly. Drop the batter by spoonfuls into the hot oil and cook until golden, about 1 minute. Use a slotted spoon to remove from the oil and drain on a layer of paper towels.

SWEET HUSH PUPPIES

serves 4

2 cups yellow cornmeal
1 tablespoon flour
1 tablespoon sugar
1 teaspoon baking powder
¾ teaspoon baking soda
1¼ cups buttermilk
1 egg, well beaten
lard or vegetable oil for deep frying
¼ cup honey
1 tablespoon lemon juice
1 lemon slice
¼ cup confectioners' sugar

•

Sift together the cornmeal, flour, sugar, baking powder and baking soda in a bowl. Beat in the buttermilk and egg.

Blend the honey with the lemon juice in a skillet or saucepan and cook over low heat. Add the lemon slice.

Fill a deep skillet to a depth of 1 inch with lard or vegetable oil and place over medium heat.

Drop the batter by heaping teaspoonfuls into the hot oil and cook until golden brown. Drain on paper towels. Dip the hush puppies into the honey and allow the excess to drain back into the pan. Place on a platter, dust with confectioners' sugar and serve.

ORANGE NUT BREAD

makes 1 bread

2 cups sifted flour
1 teaspoon baking soda
¾ teaspoon salt
½ cup sugar
1 egg, well beaten
¾ cup orange juice
2 tablespoons lemon juice
1 teaspoon grated orange rind
¼ teaspoon grated lemon rind
¼ cup solid white shortening or butter, melted
¾ cup pecan pieces

•

Butter a 9 × 5 × 3-inch loaf pan. Set aside. In a large bowl, sift together the flour, baking soda, salt and sugar.

Blend together the egg, orange juice, lemon juice, orange rind and lemon rind in a bowl. Blend in the melted shortening and pour over the dry ingredients. Blend thoroughly.

Stir in the pecans, turn into loaf pan, cover with foil or a clean towel and let stand for 20 minutes.

Preheat the oven to 350°F. Remove the cover and bake for 1 hour.

PEANUT BREAD

serves 6

½ cup sugar
3 teaspoons baking powder
4 cups flour
½ teaspoon salt
1 teaspoon baking soda
1½ cups milk
½ cup corn syrup
1 cup freshly chopped unsalted peanuts

•

Preheat the oven to 350°F. Sift together the sugar, baking powder, salt and soda in a bowl.

Combine the milk and corn syrup in another bowl. Blend the two mixtures together, then stir in the peanuts. Turn the mixture into a large buttered loaf pan and bake for 50 minutes.

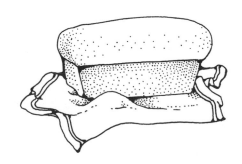

Pecan Corn Muffins

makes 18 muffins

3½ cups whole wheat flour
1 cup yellow cornmeal
1 package active dry yeast
1 teaspoon baking powder
1 teaspoon salt
1 cup milk
8 tablespoons butter
½ cup water
⅓ cup honey
2 eggs
1 cup coarsely chopped pecans

●

Grease 18 muffin-tin cups. Sprinkle each cup with a little bit of cornmeal. Set aside.

In a large bowl, combine 1 cup of the whole wheat flour, the cornmeal, yeast, baking powder and salt.

Place the milk, butter, water and honey in a saucepan. Heat the mixture until the butter melts. Set aside and cool until lukewarm.

When the milk mixture has cooled, pour it into the flour mixture. With an electric mixer, beat the batter at medium speed for 2 minutes. Beat in the eggs. Remove from mixer and stir in the remaining flour. Add the pecans and stir. The dough should be a little lumpy.

Fill each muffin cup three-quarters full with the dough. Smooth the tops. Cover the muffin tins with clean towels and let the dough rise in a warm place for 40 to 50 minutes or until the dough almost fills the tins.

Preheat the oven to 350°F.

Bake the muffins for 20 minutes or until golden brown. Serve warm.

Traditional Hush Puppies

serves 8

2 cups yellow cornmeal
1 tablespoon flour
3 teaspoons baking powder
1 teaspoon salt
1 egg, well beaten
2 cups milk
1 small onion, finely chopped
½ teaspoon cayenne pepper
lard or vegetable oil for frying

●

Sift together the cornmeal, flour, baking powder and salt in a bowl. In another bowl beat together the eggs, milk, onion and cayenne pepper. Blend the two mixtures together.

Fill a deep skillet to a depth of 1 inch with lard or vegetable oil and place over medium heat.

Drop the batter by tablespoonfuls into the hot fat and fry until golden brown. Drain on paper towels and serve.

PECAN WAFFLES

serves 6

3 cups sifted flour
3 teaspoons baking powder
2 teaspoons sugar
½ teaspoon salt
3 egg yolks, lightly beaten
1¼ cups milk
4 tablespoons melted butter
3 egg whites, stiffly beaten
¼ cup finely chopped pecans

•

Sift together the flour, baking powder, sugar and salt in a bowl. In another bowl beat together the egg yolks and milk and blend in the butter. Pour the egg yolk mixture over the dry ingredients and blend thoroughly. Gently fold in the beaten egg whites and blend. Stir in the pecans. Cook on a waffle iron until golden.

RAISIN BREAD

makes 1 loaf

1 cup applesauce
¼ cup melted butter
1 egg, beaten
½ cup sugar
¼ cup firmly packed brown sugar
2 cups sifted flour
2 teaspoons baking powder
¾ teaspoon salt
½ teaspoon baking soda
½ teaspoon cinnamon
1 teaspoon nutmeg
¾ cup seedless raisins
¾ cup chopped walnuts

•

Preheat the oven to 350°F. Combine the applesauce, butter, egg, sugar and brown sugar in a large bowl and blend well. Sift together the flour, baking powder, salt, baking soda, cinnamon and nutmeg in a bowl. Blend the two mixtures together until smooth. Stir in the raisins and walnuts and turn the batter into a well-greased loaf pan. Bake for 1 hour.

SALLY LUNN

serves 6

1 package active dry yeast
¼ cup warm water
½ cup milk, scalded
⅔ cup softened butter
2 tablespoons sugar
¾ teaspoon salt
2 cups sifted flour
2 eggs, well beaten

•

Soften the yeast in the warm water in a small bowl. Pour the scalded milk over the butter and blend in the sugar and salt. Cool slightly. Blend in ½ cup flour and beat until smooth. Stir the yeast into the batter mix and blend thoroughly. Stir in half of the remaining flour and blend well. Add the eggs and blend well. Stir in the remaining flour and blend well.

Form a ball with the batter, cover with a clean kitchen towel and let rise until it doubles in bulk (about 45 minutes).

Beat the batter again for 5 minutes. Cover and allow to stand for 45 minutes longer.

Preheat the oven to 350°F. Turn the batter into a lightly buttered ring mold or tube pan. Bake for 30 minutes, or until golden brown. Serve with loads of butter.

RICE BREAD

makes 1 loaf

1 cup cooked cold rice, pushed through a sieve
2 cups white cornmeal
3 eggs
1 tablespoon melted butter
2½ teaspoons baking powder
2¼ cups milk
1 teaspoon salt

•

Preheat the oven to 400°F.

In a bowl beat the eggs lightly. Gradually pour in the milk and mix well.

In another bowl combine the cornmeal, salt and baking powder. Add to the egg mixture and beat well. Add the melted butter and sieved rice. Beat until the batter is very light.

Butter a shallow 9 × 9-inch baking pan and fill with the batter. Bake for 30 minutes or until golden. Serve hot with butter.

SCONES

serves 4

2 cups sifted cake flour
1 tablespoon sugar
½ teaspoon salt
4 teaspoons baking powder
4 tablespoons softened butter
½ cup milk
1 egg, well beaten
¼ cup melted butter
¼ cup sugar

•

Preheat the oven to 400°F. Sift together the flour, sugar, salt and baking powder twice in a bowl. Cut in the butter with two knives and blend. Beat together the milk and egg in another bowl and blend the two mixtures together.

Form the dough into a ball and place on a floured surface. Roll the dough out into a large circle with a thickness of one-half inch, and cut into 16 wedges. Place the wedges on a buttered baking sheet and brush with the butter. Sprinkle on the sugar and bake for 15 minutes. Serve warm.

SPOON BREAD

serves 6

3 cups milk
1 cup white cornmeal
2½ tablespoons melted butter
1 teaspoon salt
3 eggs, beaten
3 teaspoons baking powder

•

Preheat the oven to 400°F. Put 2 cups of the milk in a saucepan and blend in the cornmeal and salt. Bring to a boil, reduce the heat and cook until thickened.

Beat the eggs in a bowl with the remaining milk, 1½ tablespoons of butter and baking powder.

With the remaining melted butter, grease a casserole dish. Place in the oven to preheat.

Mix the two batters together and blend well. Pour the mixture into the heated casserole dish and bake for 30 minutes.

SWEET GRIDDLECAKES

serves 4

3 cups sifted flour
3 teaspoons baking powder
½ teaspoon salt
¼ cup sugar
¼ teaspoon cinnamon
3 eggs
2 cups milk
3 tablespoons melted butter

•

Sift together the flour, baking powder, salt, sugar and cinnamon in a bowl. In another bowl beat together the eggs and milk and blend in the butter. Pour the egg mixture over the dry mixture and blend well. Spoon onto a greased griddle and cook until bubbly and firm around the edges; flip and cook the other side.

SWEET POTATO BISCUITS

makes 30 biscuits

2½ cups sifted flour
2 tablespoons baking powder
¾ teaspoon salt
½ cup cold solid white shortening
1 egg, well beaten
¾ cup milk
1½ cups mashed sweet potatoes
¼ cup light cream

•

Sift together the flour, baking powder and salt in a large bowl. Cut in the shortening with a pastry blender. Beat together the egg, milk and mashed sweet potatoes, then blend the two mixtures together thoroughly. Chill.

Preheat the oven to 400°F. Knead the dough lightly on a floured surface and roll out to a thickness of one-half inch. Cut out round, 2-inch biscuits with a floured pastry knife or cookie cutter and place on a greased baking sheet. Brush the tops with the light cream and bake for 15 minutes.

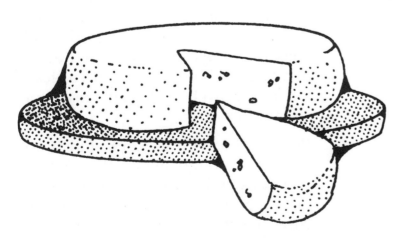

SWEET POTATO BREAD

makes 1 loaf

⅓ cup butter, softened
1 cup sugar
2 eggs, beaten
½ cup molasses
1 cup mashed sweet potatoes
2 cups sifted flour
¼ teaspoon baking powder
1 teaspoon baking soda
½ teaspoon salt
½ teaspoon cinnamon
½ teaspoon nutmeg
½ teaspoon allspice
¼ teaspoon ground cloves
¼ cup raisins
¾ cup chopped walnuts

•

Preheat the oven to 350°F. Blend together the butter, sugar, eggs, molasses and sweet potatoes in a bowl. In another bowl sift together the flour, baking powder, baking soda, salt, cinnamon, nutmeg, allspice and cloves. Combine the two mixtures, stirring until smooth, then add the raisins and walnuts. Turn the batter into a greased, medium-sized loaf pan and bake for 1 hour.

SWEET POTATO ROLLS

makes 20 rolls

1 large yam or sweet potato
1 package active dry yeast
1 teaspoon salt
3 tablespoons sugar
1 tablespoon melted butter
1 cup milk
4 cups flour, sifted

•

Pare the yam and cut into several pieces. Place in a skillet and add just enough water to cover. Bring to a boil and simmer for 20 minutes over low heat. Drain, reserving ¼ cup of the liquid. Cool the reserved liquid in a small bowl and blend in the yeast. Mash the yam in a large bowl and blend in the salt, sugar and butter.

Heat the milk in a saucepan until it is very hot but not boiling. Add the milk to the yam mixture and stir well. Add the yeast mixture and stir well again. Sift in ½ cup of the flour at a time and continue to beat until all of the flour has been added. Form the dough into a ball and place on a floured cutting board. Knead until smooth and elastic. Place the dough in a greased bowl, cover with a clean kitchen towel and let rise for 45 minutes.

Preheat the oven to 425°F. Pinch off pieces of dough about the size of golf balls and place them in greased muffin pans with a total of 20 muffin cups. Let rise again until double in size. Bake for 14 minutes.

Desserts

BANANAS FLAMBÉ

serves 4

4 firm bananas
½ cup butter
¾ cup sugar
4 tablespoons lemon juice
½ cup brandy

•

Slice the bananas in half lengthwise. Melt the butter in the top of a double boiler over simmering water. Stir in the sugar and lemon juice. Stir until the sugar is well blended.

Add the bananas and sauté for several minutes, until golden. Transfer the bananas to a serving dish and pour the brandy over them. Carefully ignite the brandy with a match. Spoon the sauce over the bananas until the flame dies out.

BLACKBERRY CAKE

makes 1 cake

1½ cups sugar
½ cup butter
2 eggs
1 cup fresh blackberries
2 cups flour
½ teaspoon baking powder
1 teaspoon grated nutmeg
½ teaspoon cinnamon
⅔ cup buttermilk
1 teaspoon baking soda

•

Preheat the oven to 350°F. Butter and flour a 13 × 9 × 2-inch baking pan. Set aside.

In a mixing bowl combine the sugar, butter, eggs and blackberries. Beat the mixture with an electric mixer at medium-high for 2 minutes.

In a separate bowl combine the flour, baking powder, nutmeg and cinnamon.

Combine the buttermilk and baking soda in a bowl. Add alternately with the flour mixture to the berries. Beat for 2 minutes.

Pour the batter into the pan and bake for 25 to 30 minutes, or until a cake tester inserted into the center of the cake comes out clean.

Remove and let cool. Serve from baking pan.

Pecan Pie

Pink Lemonade

Chow-Chow

BRANDIED WHOLE PEACHES

makes approximately 6 pints

**4 pounds sugar
4 pounds ripe, unblemished whole
peaches
2 cups brandy**

•

In a large pot place the sugar and add enough water to dissolve. Bring the mixture to a boil. Add the peaches and cook for 5 minutes.

Remove the peaches and boil the syrup 15 minutes longer. Stir in the brandy. Remove the pot from the heat.

Place the peaches into six 1-pint sterilized jars. Pour the syrup over them. Seal, cool, and store.

BROILED FRUIT WITH RUM SAUCE

serves 6

**½ cup brown sugar
¼ cup dark rum
4 bananas, halved lengthwise
1 small pineapple, peeled and cubed
½ pound seedless grapes
2 apples, cored and sliced
¼ pound coarsely chopped walnuts**

•

Combine the brown sugar and rum in a saucepan and cook over moderate heat, stirring constantly until the sugar has melted.

Preheat the broiler. Arrange the fruit in a broiler pan and sprinkle with the walnuts. Pour the sauce over the fruit and broil for 3 minutes.

CHARLESTON TORTE

makes 1 torte

3 eggs
1½ cups sugar
¼ cup flour
1 teaspoon baking powder
¼ teaspoon salt
1 cup finely chopped apples
1 cup finely chopped pecans
1 teaspoon pure vanilla extract
1 cup chilled heavy cream
2 tablespoons chopped pecans

•

Preheat the oven to 400°F. Generously butter a 12 × 8 × 2-inch baking pan. Set aside.

Sift together the flour, baking powder and salt. Set aside.

Beat the eggs briefly. Then add the sugar and vanilla and beat until the mixture is thick, about 4 to 5 minutes.

Beat in the flour mixture until well blended. Add the chopped apples and the chopped pecans. Mix them gently but thoroughly into the batter with a rubber spatula.

Turn the batter into the pan and bake for 30 to 35 minutes, or until a cake tester inserted into the center comes out clean.

Remove the cake from the oven and cool slightly.

Beat the cream in a chilled mixing bowl until it is stiff. Transfer the cream to a serving bowl and sprinkle it with the 2 tablespoons chopped pecans. Serve the cake directly from the baking pan while it is still warm. Serve the whipped cream on the side.

BROWN SUGAR PIE

makes 1 pie

1 cup firmly packed brown sugar
1 egg, slightly beaten
2 tablespoons flour
3 tablespoons milk
1 teaspoon pure vanilla extract
2 tablespoons melted butter
1 pastry for 9-inch pie

•

Preheat the oven to 350°F.

Roll the pie pastry out onto a lightly floured suface. Fit it into pie shell and flute edges. Set aside.

In a large bowl combine the brown sugar, egg, flour, milk, vanilla extract and melted butter. Mix until well blended.

Pour the mixture into the pie shell. Bake for 15 minutes or until set. Remove from the oven and let cool. Serve warm.

CASHEW SHORTBREAD

makes 4 dozen

2 cups sifted flour
½ teaspoon baking powder
1 cup butter
½ cup confectioners' sugar
1 cup salted chopped cashews

•

Sift the flour and baking powder together in a bowl. In another bowl cream the butter until soft and work in the sugar until smooth. Stir in the flour and blend well. Stir in the cashews. Chill for 1 hour.

Preheat the oven to 375°F. Divide the dough in half and roll out each half to a thickness of one-half inch. Cut the dough into 1½-inch squares and place on an ungreased baking sheet. Bake for 15 minutes.

CIDER CAKE

serves 6

3 cups sifted flour
½ teaspoon baking soda
¼ teaspoon salt
½ teaspoon grated nutmeg
½ cup melted butter
1½ cups sugar
2 eggs, beaten
½ cup cider

•

Preheat the oven to 350°F. Butter a 10-inch tube pan.

Sift together the flour, baking soda, salt and nutmeg in a bowl. In another bowl stir the butter and sugar together until all the sugar has dissolved. Beat the eggs into the sugar. Add the flour mixture and cider to the sugar mixture and blend thoroughly.

Turn the mixture into the prepared pan and bake for 1 hour.

COCONUT DELIGHT

serves 8

1 pound grated coconut
8 large scoops vanilla ice cream
8 jiggers (12 ounces) crème de menthe

•

Preheat the broiler. Sprinkle the coconut on a baking sheet and toast under the broiler for 1 to 2 minutes.

Scoop the ice cream into chilled sundae dishes or small clear glasses. Sprinkle with the coconut and pour one jigger of crème de menthe over each serving and freeze. Cover with wax paper for 1 hour before serving.

CREOLE KISSES

makes 4 dozen

3 egg whites
2 cups confectioners' sugar
1 teaspoon vanilla extract
½ cup chopped pecans

•

Preheat the oven to 350°F. Beat the egg whites in a bowl until stiff and able to hold peaks, then beat in the sugar and vanilla extract, a little at a time. Stir in the pecans.

Cover a baking sheet with brown wrapping paper and drop the batter by the teaspoonful onto the paper. Bake for 17 minutes.

COCONUT JUMBLES

makes approximately 36 cookies

⅔ cup butter
1 cup sugar
1 egg, beaten
1 cup flour
1 cup freshly grated coconut

•

Preheat the oven to 375°F. Heavily grease two baking sheets and set aside.

Cream the butter in a large mixing bowl. Add the sugar and continue creaming until the mixture is light and fluffy. Add the egg and mix well. Stir in the flour and mix well. Gradually add the coconut and mix until the batter is stiff.

Drop the batter by well-rounded teaspoons onto the baking sheets. Bake for 5 to 7 minutes, or until the cookies are lightly browned.

Cool the cookies for 30 seconds on the baking sheets and then remove to cooling racks. Cool completely.

CREAM CHEESE SOUFFLÉ WITH BLACK CHERRY SAUCE

serves 8

SOUFFLÉ:
8 ounces cream cheese, softened
1 cup sour cream
1 tablespoon honey
¼ teaspoon salt
3 egg yolks, beaten
3 egg whites
2 tablespoons sugar

SAUCE:
¾ cup orange juice
2 tablespoons sugar
1 tablespoon cornstarch
¼ cup water
1 8-ounce can black cherries, with juice
3 tablespoons brandy

•

Preheat the oven to 420°F. Butter a 1½-quart soufflé or casserole dish.

Whip the cream cheese, sour cream, honey, salt and egg yolks with a mixer until smooth.

Beat the egg whites in a bowl until stiff peaks are formed. Gradually add the sugar, continuing to beat until the whites are stiff again. Blend the whites into the cream cheese mixture. Pour the mixture into the soufflé dish. Bake for 45 minutes.

To make the sauce, heat the orange juice in the top of a double boiler over simmering water. Blend in the sugar. Combine the cornstarch and water in a small bowl and blend thoroughly. Add to the orange juice.

Cook until the sauce is thick and then stir in the cherries and their juice. Continue to cook for 5 minutes more. Stir in the brandy and remove from the stove. Serve the soufflé immediately with some sauce spooned over each serving.

FOX HEAD PIE

serves 12

1 cup sugar
4 eggs, slightly beaten
1 cup corn syrup
1 teaspoon vanilla extract
¼ pound melted butter
1¼ cups chopped walnuts
1¼ cups semisweet chocolate chips
2 8-inch pie shells

•

Preheat the oven to 325°F. Blend together the sugar, eggs, syrup, vanilla and butter in a mixing bowl. Stir in the walnuts and chocolate chips. Divide the mixture among the pie shells. Bake for 40 minutes or until set. Cool and serve. *As supplied by Elizabeth Harakas.*

FUDGE

makes 1 pound

**2 cups sugar
2 ounces (2 squares) unsweetened
chocolate, grated
1 cup light cream
1 tablespoon butter**

•

Combine the sugar, chocolate and cream in a saucepan and cook over moderate heat, stirring constantly, just until sugar and chocolate have melted. Continue to cook until the mixture has reached 240°F on a candy thermometer. Remove from the heat and beat in the butter. Continue to beat until the fudge begins to harden. Turn onto a buttered platter, spread evenly, and cut into small squares before the fudge has hardened.

HONEY CUSTARD

serves 6

**3 eggs
½ cup honey
⅛ teaspoon salt
2¾ cups milk
½ teaspoon lemon extract
½ teaspoon grated orange rind
½ teaspoon nutmeg**

•

Preheat the oven to 350°F. Beat the eggs in a bowl until they are light and blend in the honey. Continue to beat until well beaten. Scald the milk and slowly pour milk into egg mixture, stirring constantly. Blend in the lemon extract and orange rind and pour into buttered custard cups.

Sprinkle with the nutmeg and place the custard cups into a baking pan filled with water to a depth of 1 inch. Bake for 45 minutes or until set. Cool slightly and serve, or refrigerate and serve cold.

HUCKLEBERRY PIE

serves 6 to 8

1 quart fresh huckleberries
3 tablespoons quick-cooking tapioca
1 cup sugar
¼ teaspoon salt
juice of 1 lemon
1 pastry for 2-crust, 9-inch pie
1 tablespoon butter, cut into pieces

•

Preheat the oven to 450°F.

In a large bowl combine the huckleberries, tapioca, sugar, salt and lemon juice. Set aside.

Roll out the pastry on a lightly floured surface. Fit half of it into a 9-inch pie plate. Trim the edges.

Pour the berry mixture into the pie shell. Dot with butter.

Cover the pie with the remaining pastry. Moisten the edges with a little water and flute to seal. Cut several vents in the top.

Bake the pie for 10 minutes. Reduce the heat to 350°F and bake for 30 to 35 minutes longer. Serve warm or cold.

FRUIT FROSTING

makes enough for 1 2-layer cake

½ cup pitted dates
1½ cups raisins
1 orange, peeled
1 lemon, peeled
⅓ cup sugar

•

Grind the dates and raisins together and place them in a saucepan. Cut the orange and lemon into pieces and remove all the seeds. Grind the pieces together and add them to the saucepan.

Add the sugar to the saucepan and cook over medium heat until the mixture thickens. Stir constantly. Spread the frosting over the cake while still warm.

To frost the jam cake, place one cake layer top-side down on a serving plate. Brush off any crumbs. Spread with about one-third the frosting mixture. Place the second layer, top-side up, on top. Frost the sides of both layers and then frost the top. Smooth the frosting. Allow the frosting to set for a few hours before cutting the cake.

JAM CAKE

makes 1 cake

¾ cup softened butter
1 cup sugar
3 eggs
3 cups flour
2 teaspoons baking powder
1 teaspoon baking soda
¼ teaspoon salt
1 teaspoon ground cinnamon
½ cup buttermilk
1 cup thick blackberry jam

•

Preheat the oven to 350°F. Grease two 9-inch round cake pans. Set aside.

In a large mixing bowl cream the butter and sugar until light and fluffy. Add the eggs and beat well.

In a bowl or on a large sheet of wax paper, sift together the flour, baking powder, baking soda and cinnamon three times.

Add the flour mixture to the creamed mixture alternately with the buttermilk. End with the flour. Fold in the jam.

Turn the batter into the prepared cake pans. Distribute it evenly. Bake the cakes for 35 to 45 minutes, or until they are golden brown.

Remove the cakes to cooling racks and cool in the pans for 10 minutes. Turn out onto racks and continue cooling.

Frost with Fruit Frosting

KENTUCKY BOURBON CAKE

serves 8

¾ pound softened butter
2½ cups firmly packed brown sugar
2 cups sugar
6 eggs
5½ cups sifted flour
1 teaspoon mace
¼ teaspoon salt
2 cups bourbon whiskey
1 pound pecans, coarsely chopped

•

Preheat the oven to 300°F. Butter a 10-inch tube pan.

Beat the butter in a bowl until soft and smooth. Combine the white and brown sugar in a bowl. Blend half of the combined sugars into the butter and mix well.

Beat the eggs in a bowl and then beat in the remaining sugar. Blend the sugar mixtures. Sift together the flour, mace and salt. Add the flour mixture and whiskey to the sugar mixture and blend well. Stir in the pecans. Turn the batter into the prepared pan and bake for 1½ hours.

KENTUCKY BOURBON BALLS

makes about 50 balls

1 6-ounce package semisweet chocolate
pieces
½ cup sugar
2 tablespoons light corn syrup
⅓ cup bourbon whiskey
7 ounces finely ground vanilla wafers
1 cup finely chopped walnuts
1 cup finely ground pecans or almonds

•

In the top of a double boiler over hot but not boiling water, melt the chocolate pieces.

Remove the double boiler from the heat and stir in the sugar, corn syrup and bourbon whiskey.

In a mixing bowl combine the wafer crumbs and the walnuts. Stir in the chocolate mixture. Blend well.

Immediately shape the mixture into 1-inch balls and roll them in the ground pecans.

Store in an airtight container for at least 7 days before serving.

KENTUCKY COLONELS

makes 20 candies

4 tablespoons softened butter
2 cups confectioners' sugar
3 tablespoons bourbon whiskey
⅓ cup finely chopped pecans
8 ounces (8 squares) semisweet
chocolate

•

In the top of a double boiler over hot but not boiling water, melt the chocolate. Remove from the heat and cool.

Cream the butter and sugar together in a mixing bowl until light and fluffy. Beat in the bourbon whiskey, 1 tablespoon at a time. Add the completely cooled chocolate. Mix well. Stir in the pecans.

Line a baking sheet with waxed paper.

Form the candies by taking 1 tablespoon of the mixture at a time and rolling it between the palms. Place the balls on the lined baking sheet.

Refrigerate for 45 minutes or until firm.

KENTUCKY EGGNOG

serves 30

24 egg yolks
1½ cups sugar
1½ cups dark rum
6 cups bourbon whiskey
1 quart whipped heavy cream
1 quart vanilla ice cream

•

Beat the egg yolks in the bowl of an electric mixer until they are light. Beat in the sugar, and continue to beat for 20 minutes. Stir in the rum and allow the mixture to stand for 1 hour.

Stir in the bourbon whiskey and let stand 10 minutes. Fold in the whipped cream and pour the eggnog into a large chilled punch bowl. Break up the ice cream into chunks and float them in the eggnog. Stir gently and serve.

LIME CHIFFON PIE

serves 6

1 envelope unflavored gelatin
¼ cup cold water
4 egg yolks, slightly beaten
⅔ cup sugar
2 teaspoons grated lime rind
½ cup lime juice
¼ teaspoon salt
3 drops green food coloring
4 egg whites
½ cup sugar
1 baked 10-inch pie shell

•

Dissolve the gelatin in the cold water in a small bowl. Set aside.

Blend together the egg yolks, sugar, lime rind, lime juice and salt in the top of a double boiler and simmer over boiling water for 10 minutes, stirring constantly. Remove from the heat and stir in the gelatin. Stir until the gelatin is well dissolved. Blend in the food coloring.

Beat the whites in a bowl until stiff and then gradually add the sugar continually beating until peaks are formed. Turn the stiff whites into the gelatin mixture and mix thoroughly. Turn the mixture into the pie shell and chill until set.

ORANGE PECAN CAKE

serves 6

6 eggs, separated
1 cup solid white vegetable shortening
2 cups sugar
4 cups sifted cake flour
1 teaspoon baking powder
¼ teaspoon salt
½ teaspoon baking soda
1 teaspoon nutmeg
1 cup orange juice
3 cups chopped pecans
1 pound seedless raisins
2 egg whites
1½ cups sugar
¼ cup water
1½ teaspoons corn syrup
juice and grated rind of ½ orange
whole pecans

•

Preheat the oven to 325°F. Line a 10-inch tube pan with waxed paper. Beat the egg whites in a bowl until stiff. Set aside.

Beat the shortening in a mixing bowl until softened. Add the sugar gradually, creaming until the sugar is completely dissolved. Add the egg yolks and beat thoroughly. Sift together the flour, baking powder, salt and baking soda in a bowl and blend into the yolk mixture with the orange juice. Blend well. Fold in the reserved egg whites. Stir in the pecans and raisins and turn into the prepared tube pan. Bake for 1½ hours.

Twenty minutes before the cake has finished baking, make the icing. Blend the 2 egg whites, sugar, water and corn syrup in the top of a double boiler. Cook over boiling water, beating constantly, for 7 minutes. Remove from heat and continue to beat, gradually adding the orange juice and rind, until the icing is cool enough to spread.

Remove the cake from the oven, allow to cool slightly, frost and garnish with whole pecans.

MAPLE GINGERBREAD

serves 6

2⅓ cups flour, sifted
1 teaspoon baking soda
1½ teaspoons ground ginger
½ teaspoon salt
1 egg
1 cup maple syrup
1 cup sour cream
4 tablespoons melted butter

ICING:
2 cups confectioners' sugar
⅛ teaspoon salt
1 tablespoon softened butter
3 tablespoons maple syrup
1 tablespoon heavy cream

●

Preheat the oven to 350°F. Butter an 11 × 7 × 1½-inch baking pan. Sift together the flour, baking soda, ginger and salt in a bowl. In another bowl beat the egg and blend in the maple syrup, sour cream and butter. Blend the two mixtures together and turn into the prepared pan. Bake for 30 minutes.

To make the icing, combine the confectioners' sugar, butter, maple syrup and cream in a bowl. Beat until smooth and spreadable.

Remove the cake from the oven and cool. Frost and serve.

OSGOOD PIE

makes 1 pie

½ cup butter
1 cup sugar
2 eggs, separated
½ cup chopped pecans
½ cup raisins
½ teaspoon ground cloves
½ teaspoon cinnamon
2 teaspoons cocoa
1 teaspoon vinegar
1 pastry for 9-inch pie

●

Preheat the oven to 375°F.

Roll the pastry out onto a lightly floured surface. Fit it into a 9-inch pie plate and flute the edges. Set aside.

In a large bowl cream the butter and sugar together until they are light and fluffy. Beat the egg yolks and add them to the creamed mixture. Blend well.

Stir in the pecans, raisins, cloves, cinnamon, cocoa and vinegar. Mix well.

In a small bowl, beat the egg whites until they are stiff but not dry. Fold the egg whites into the sugar mixture.

Turn the mixture into the pie shell and bake for 10 minutes. Reduce the heat to 325°F and bake for 30 minutes longer. Cool before serving.

PEACH COBBLER

serves 6

⅔ cup sugar
⅓ cup water
1 tablespoon flour
3 cups fresh peach slices
4 tablespoons softened butter
¾ teaspoon cinnamon
1½ cups flour, sifted
1 tablespoon baking powder
¼ teaspoon salt
3 tablespoons butter
½ cup milk

•

Blend the water and sugar in a skillet and simmer over low heat for 2 minutes. Stir in the flour and simmer for 1 minute. Stir in the peach slices and simmer for 5 minutes, stirring constantly.

Preheat the oven to 425°F. Butter an 8-inch square baking pan.

Pour the peach mixture into the prepared pan. Sprinkle with the cinnamon and dot with the butter. In a bowl sift the flour, baking powder and salt together. Cut in the butter and blend in the milk. Beat until a ball is formed. Transfer the dough to a floured surface and knead for 3 minutes. Roll the dough out into a square about 8½ × 8½ inches, large enough to cover the pan. Cover the peaches with the pastry and pinch the batter to the edges of the pan. Bake for 25 minutes. Serve warm.

PEACH SHERBET

makes 1 quart

1 dozen ripe peaches
1 pound sugar
1 quart water
½ cup lemon juice

•

Peel the peaches and halve them. Remove the pits. Cut the peaches into small pieces and place them in a bowl. Sprinkle with 1 cup of the sugar and mash with a fork. Set aside for 1 hour.

In a saucepan bring the water, remaining sugar and lemon juice to a boil. Boil for 5 minutes and remove the syrup from the heat. Set aside to cool.

When the syrup is cooled, add the peaches and mix well. Press the mixture through a fine sieve. Extract as much juice as possible from the peaches.

Pour the mixture into a chilled electric ice cream machine and churn, following the manufacturer's directions, until the mixture is firm, about 15 minutes.

Serve immediately or freeze. The sherbet will keep well in a covered container in the freezer for 1 week. Remove from the freezer 10 to 15 minutes before serving.

PEACH FRITTERS

serves 8

1 cup sifted flour
2 tablespoons sugar
¼ teaspoon salt
⅔ cup milk
2 eggs, separated
2 tablespoons melted butter
6 large ripe peaches, peeled, halved,
pitted and cut into wedges
3 tablespoons lemon juice
vegetable oil for frying

•

Sift together the flour, sugar and salt in a bowl. In another bowl beat together the milk, egg yolks and butter. Blend the two mixtures. Beat the egg whites until stiff in a bowl and fold into the batter. Stir well.

Toss the peach wedges with the lemon juice in a bowl. Dip the peaches in the batter. Fill a large heavy skillet with oil to a depth of 1 inch. Heat until the oil is very hot, 365°F. Fry the coated peach wedges in the oil until golden on all sides. Drain on paper towels and dust with confectioners' sugar.

PEANUT BUTTER SNACKS

serves 8

32 Ritz crackers
32 tablespoons smooth peanut butter
32 large marshmallows

•

Preheat the broiler. Place the crackers on a baking sheet and spread each with 1 tablespoon of peanut butter. Top each cracker with a marshmallow and place under the broiler for 2 minutes.

PECAN BUTTER BALLS

makes 36 cookies

½ cup butter
2 tablespoons sugar
1 teaspoon pure vanilla extract
1 cup flour
⅛ teaspoon salt
1 cup finely ground pecans
confectioner's sugar

•

Preheat the oven to 375°F.

In a large bowl cream the butter and sugar together until they are light and fluffy. Add the vanilla and mix well. Add the flour and salt to the creamed mixture and mix well. Add the nuts and stir until thoroughly combined.

Drop the batter by well-rounded teaspoons onto ungreased baking sheets. Bake for 20 minutes.

Remove the balls from the oven and cool for 1 minute on the baking sheets. Roll each ball in confectioner's sugar and continue cooling. Store in the refrigerator.

PECAN PIE

serves 6

1 8-inch pie shell
3 eggs
¼ teaspoon salt
¾ cup sugar
½ cup melted butter
1 cup dark corn syrup
1½ cups pecan halves

•

Preheat the oven to 450°F then bake the pie shell for 5 minutes. Remove the pie shell. Reduce the heat to 425°F.

Beat the eggs and salt in a bowl. Beat in the sugar. Fold in the butter and syrup and turn into the pie shell. Cover the surface of the pies with the pecans and bake for 10 minutes. Reduce the heat to 325°F and continue to bake for 30 minutes.

PRALINES

makes 2 dozen

3 cups firmly packed light brown sugar
¼ cup water
1 tablespoon butter
1 cup coarsely chopped pecans

•

Combine the sugar, water and butter in a saucepan and cook over low heat, stirring, until the mixture has reached 240°F on a candy thermometer. Stir in the pecans until the mixture adheres to the nuts.

Remove from the heat and continue to stir until candy is opaque. Drop by the tablespoon onto waxed paper, making small patties and let harden.

SOUR CREAM COOKIES

makes 8 dozen

1 cup softened butter
2 cups firmly packed brown sugar
1 cup sour cream
3 eggs, beaten
1 teaspoon pure vanilla extract
4 cups sifted flour
2 teaspoons baking soda
1 teaspoon grated nutmeg
½ teaspoon salt

•

Preheat the oven to 350°F. Cream the butter in a bowl and blend in the sugar. Beat in the sour cream, eggs and vanilla.

Sift together the flour, soda, nutmeg and salt in another bowl. Blend the two mixtures together. Drop by spoonfuls onto a greased baking sheet and bake for 12 minutes.

PECAN COOKIES

makes 3 dozen

2 egg whites
1 cup firmly packed brown sugar
½ teaspoon maple flavoring
1 cup chopped pecans
1 cup fine unflavored breadcrumbs
¼ teaspoon salt

•

Preheat the oven to 325°F. Beat the egg whites in a bowl until stiff but not dry. Beat in the sugar and maple flavoring. Mix the pecans, breadcrumbs and salt in a bowl and fold into the batter. Form the dough into 36 small balls and place on a greased baking sheet. Bake for 20 minutes.

PECAN NOUGAT

makes 4 cups

1½ cups coarsely chopped pecans
2 cups sugar
2 tablespoons lemon juice

•

Preheat the oven to 350°F. Toast the pecans on a baking sheet for 15 minutes.

Combine the sugar and lemon juice in a heavy skillet and cook over low heat, stirring constantly, until sugar has melted and turned golden brown. Stir in the pecans and pour onto a greased baking sheet. Spread quickly with an oiled spatula and allow to harden. Break into pieces.

PECAN-TOPPED PUMPKIN PIE

serves 6

2 cups mashed cooked pumpkin
⅔ cup firmly packed brown sugar
1 teaspoon cinnamon
½ teaspoon ground ginger
½ teaspoon grated nutmeg
⅛ teaspoon ground cloves
½ teaspoon salt
2 eggs, slightly beaten
2 cups light cream, scalded
1 9-inch pastry shell
3 tablespoons butter
1 cup pecan halves
¼ cup brown sugar

•

Preheat the oven to 400°F. Blend together the mashed pumpkin and ⅔ cup brown sugar in a bowl until smooth. Blend in the cinnamon, ginger, nutmeg, cloves and salt. Blend in eggs and scalded milk and fold into the pastry shell. Bake for 50 minutes.

Melt the butter in a skillet and sauté the pecan halves until well coated with the butter. Turn into a bowl with the ¼ cup brown sugar and toss until well covered.

When the pie is done, remove from the oven and turn on broiler. Arrange the pecan halves around the rim of the pie and place under the broiler for 2 minutes.

STRAWBERRY FRAPPE

serves 4

1 pint heavy cream
1 quart strawberries
¼ cup confectioners' sugar
1 jigger (1½ ounces) brandy

●

Place the strawberries in a bowl and cover with the sugar. Allow to stand for 1 hour. Drain and reserve the juice.

Whip the cream in a bowl until stiff. Blend the strawberries with the cream and chill. Blend the brandy with the reserved strawberry juice in a bowl and pour over the mixture just before serving.

SWEET POTATO PUDDING

serves 4

3 cups grated sweet potatoes
2 eggs, beaten
1½ cups molasses
½ cup brown sugar
1 cup milk
2 tablespoons flour
½ cup butter
½ teaspoon ground ginger
½ teaspoon ground cinnamon
½ teaspoon grated nutmeg
1 teaspoon ground allspice
1 teaspoon grated orange rind
1 cup whipped cream

●

Preheat the oven to 350°F. Blend all the ingredients, except the cream, thoroughly in a mixing bowl. Turn into a heavy iron skillet until thickened. Place the skillet in the oven and bake for 20 minutes. Allow to cool slightly and serve with the whipped cream.

SOUR CREAM RAISIN PIE

serves 6

2 eggs
¾ cup sugar
¼ teaspoon salt
1 teaspoon ground cinnamon
½ teaspoon grated nutmeg
¼ teaspoon ground cloves
1 cup sour cream
1 cup seedless raisins
1 10-inch pastry shell, chilled

●

Preheat the oven to 450°F. Beat the eggs in a bowl and beat in the sugar, salt, cinnamon, nutmeg and cloves. Stir in the sour cream and raisins and turn into the pie shell. Bake for 10 minutes, then reduce the heat to 350°F and bake for 30 minutes longer.

SPICED PEACHES IN BRANDY

serves 6

**12 canned, large whole peaches, pits
removed, reserving juice
12 cloves
1 blade mace
1 cinnamon stick
1 cup brandy**

●

Place the peaches and their juices in a deep skillet and put a clove in each peach. Add the mace and cinnamon stick and simmer, covered, for 15 minutes.

Use a slotted spoon to transfer the peaches to a glass casserole dish and cover with the brandy. Simmer the juice in the skillet until reduced by half. Remove the blade of mace and cinnamon stick and pour over the peaches and brandy. Cover and refrigerate for 2 days before serving.

BEVERAGES

ALABAZAM

serves 1

2 tablespoons lemon juice
1 teaspoon sugar
6 drops Angostura bitters
¾ cup crushed ice
1 jigger (1½ ounces) brandy
1 pony (1 ounce) Curaçao
sparkling water

•

Combine the lemon juice, sugar, crushed ice and bitters in a cocktail shaker. Shake well. Add the brandy and Curaçao and shake again. Strain into a tall glass. Fill the glass to the top with sparkling water, stir and serve.

CAFÉ BRÛLOT

serves 4

rinds of 2 oranges
rinds of 2 lemons
1 cinnamon stick
12 whole cloves
6 tablespoons sugar
1 cup brandy
1 cup orange liqueur
2 cups hot strong coffee

•

Remove as much white pith from the orange and lemon rinds as possible. Cut the rinds into thin slivers. Combine the rinds, cinnamon, cloves, sugar, brandy and liqueur in chafing dish over canned heat. Stir until the sugar dissolves. Carefully ignite the spirits with a match. Gradually stir in the coffee as the spirits burn. Continue mixing gently until the flames die. Serve in demitasse cups.

CLARET CUP PUNCH

makes 1 gallon

3 tablespoons sugar
1½ teaspoons grated lemon rind
3 lemon slices
1 tablespoon Angostura bitters
1 strip cucumber peel
½ jigger (¾ ounce) brandy
½ jigger (¾ ounce) cherry brandy
½ jigger (¾ ounce) white Curaçao
1 quart cold sparkling water
2 bottles chilled dry red wine
6 mint sprigs

•

Combine the sugar, lemon rind, lemon slices, bitters, cucumber peel, brandy, cherry brandy and Curaçao in a bowl, cover and let stand for 1 hour.

Place a block of ice in a chilled large punch bowl. Strain the brandy mixture into the punch bowl. Add the sparkling water, wine and mint sprigs and stir well.

EMILY'S SUNDAY PUNCH

makes 2 quarts

1 quart lime sherbet, softened
1 liter lemon-flavored soda
6 pineapple rings
12 maraschino cherries

•

Remove the sherbet whole from the container, and place it into a punch bowl. Use a large knife to slice the sherbet into four pieces.

Pour the soda over the top of the sherbet and gently stir with a large spoon until it begins to melt. Float in the pineapple rings and cherries and serve.

As you run out of liquid but still have chunks of sherbet left, add more soda to the punch bowl.

MINT JULEP

serves 1

5 mint sprigs
½ cup crushed ice
2 jiggers (3 ounces) bourbon whiskey
1 teaspoon sugar
1 teaspoon water

•

Place the mint sprigs in the bottom of a chilled goblet. Cover the sprigs with the crushed ice and pour in the bourbon whiskey. Stir gently until there is moisture on the goblet.

Mix one teaspoon of sugar with one teaspoon of water. Allow the sugar to dissolve, then stir the sweet water into the bourbon. Serve at once with a napkin wrapped around the stem of the glass.

HOT BUTTERED RUM

serves 1

1 teaspoon sugar
1 tablespoon hot water
⅛ teaspoon ground allspice
2 whole cloves
1½ ounces rum
¼ cup hot water
1 teaspoon unsalted butter

•

Dissolve the sugar in a mug with the tablespoon of hot water. Stir in the allspice, cloves and rum. Add the hot water and remove the cloves. Stir in the butter and serve.

HOT WHISKEY TODDY

serves 1

1 teaspoon sugar
½ cup boiling water
1 jigger (1½ ounces) whiskey
small twist lemon peel
grated nutmeg

•

Dissolve the sugar in the boiling water in a large mug. Add the whiskey and stir. Run the lemon twist around the rim of the mug and drop it into the drink. Sprinkle the nutmeg and serve hot.

BAYOU TODDY

serves 1

1 teaspoon sugar
½ cup boiling water
½ lemon slice
3 whole cloves
1 small cinnamon stick
¼ cup rum
grated nutmeg

•

Combine the sugar and boiling water in a mug and stir until the sugar is dissolved. Add the lemon, cloves, cinnamon stick and rum. Stir and let stand 2 minutes. Remove the cinnamon stick and cloves with a spoon. Sprinkle with nutmeg and serve.

MISSISSIPPI EGGNOG

serves 4

3 eggs, separated
¼ cup sugar
1 cup whiskey
½ cup rum
2 cups whipped cream

•

Beat the egg yolks until creamy in a bowl. Slowly add the sugar, beating constantly. Set aside.

Combine the whiskey and rum in another bowl. Slowly stir in the sweetened egg yolks. Add the whipped cream and set aside. Beat the egg whites in a bowl until they are stiff. Fold the beaten egg whites into the egg yolk mixture. Serve at once in 10-ounce glasses.

MISSISSIPPI PUNCH

serves 2

4 ounces brandy
2 ounces dark rum
2 ounces bourbon whiskey
2 ounces water
1½ tablespoons powdered sugar
2 orange slices

•

Combine the brandy, rum, bourbon, water and powdered sugar in a blender. Process on low setting for 10 seconds.

Fill two 8-ounce glasses with shaved ice and hang a slice of orange on the rim of each glass. Divide the liquid among the two glasses and serve.

MOCHA CREAM COFFEE PUNCH

makes 2 quarts

**4 cups very strong cold coffee
1½ pints chocolate ice cream, softened
¾ cup heavy cream
½ teaspoon almond extract
½ teaspoon grated nutmeg**

•

Place half the ice cream in a well-chilled punch bowl. Add the chilled coffee and stir until the ice cream begins to blend into the coffee. Set aside.

Whip the cream in a large bowl with the almond extract. Heap the whipped cream into the center of the punch bowl. Sprinkle the top of the cream with the nutmeg.

Divide the remaining ice cream among the serving glasses and ladle the coffee punch over the ice cream. *As supplied by Dorothy and Sharlyn Davis.*

RAMOS FIZZ

serves 1

**1 heaping teaspoon confectioners'
sugar
2 teaspoons lemon juice
¼ teaspoon orange flower water
1 egg white
1 ounce dry gin
2½ ounces milk
4 ounces shaved ice**

•

Combine all the ingredients in a blender. Process on low for 5 minutes. Strain into an 8-ounce glass and serve.

ROBERT E. LEE COOLER

serves 1

**1 jigger (1½ ounces) bourbon whiskey
1 tablespoon lime juice
2 dashes Pernod
6 ounces ginger ale**

•

Combine the lime juice and Pernod and stir.

Combine the whiskey, lime juice and Pernod in a mixing glass and stir gently. Pour the mixture into a tall glass filled with crushed ice. Add the ginger ale and stir gently. Serve.

PINK LEMONADE

makes 1 quart

3 large lemons
¾ cup sugar
12 ice cubes
3 cups cold water
½ bottle maraschino cherries, with
juice

•

Scrub the lemons well and trim off the ends. Cut the lemons into very thin slices, discarding the seeds, and place in a large bowl.

Sprinkle the sugar over the lemon slices, and press the sugar, hard, into the lemon slices with the back of a wooden spoon, until the sugar has dissolved.

Add the ice cubes, water, and maraschino cherry juice and stir gently. Strain into tall glasses filled with shaved ice and garnish each serving with a maraschino cherry.

PLANTERS' PUNCH

serves 1

1 orange slice
1 pineapple ring
1 tablespoon sugar
3 tablespoons water
2 jiggers (3 ounces) rum
2 tablespoons lime juice
1 cup crushed ice

•

Put the orange slice in a champagne glass, then top it with the pineapple ring. Set aside.

Combine the sugar and water in a cocktail shaker and stir until the sugar is dissolved. Add the rum and lime juice and then add the crushed ice. Cover and shake well. Strain the liquid into the champagne glass and serve.

SOUTHERN ICED TEA

makes 1 gallon

1¼ gallons water
8 teabags
1 cinnamon stick
1 pound sugar

•

Heat the water in a large cooking pot on medium-high heat. As the water begins to boil, add the tea bags and cinnamon stick. Reduce the heat to medium-low and simmer, partially covered, for 20 minutes.

Remove from heat and stir in the sugar. Stir constantly until all the sugar has dissolved. Remove the teabags and cinnamon stick and transfer to a gallon jug to refrigerate.

For lemon-flavored tea, slice up one large lemon and add it with the teabags. Remove the lemon slices with the cinnamon sticks and teabags.

SUISSESSE

serves 1

1 teaspoon sugar
2 ounces sparkling water
1 pony (1 ounce) dry vermouth
2 ponies (2 ounces) Pernod
1 egg white
crushed ice
2 tablespoons green crème de menthe
maraschino cherry

•

Combine the sugar, sparkling water, vermouth, Pernod, crushed ice and egg white in a cocktail shaker. Cover and shake well.

Place the maraschino cherry in a champagne glass and pour the crème de menthe over it. Strain the mixture over the crème de menthe and serve.

TRADITIONAL OLD-FASHIONED

serves 1

1 jigger (1½ ounces) bourbon whiskey
1 pony (1 ounce) ice water
1 dash bitters
1 twist lemon peel

•

Combine the bourbon whiskey, water and bitters in a small glass and stir gently. Run the lemon twist around the edge of the glass and drop it into the drink. Do not add ice to this drink.

VIRGINIA GRAPE COOLER

makes 1½ quarts

½ cup sugar
2 cups cold water
1 cup white grape juice
1 cup orange juice
½ cup lemon juice

•

Combine the sugar and water in a large pitcher. Stir until the sugar dissolves. Add the grape juice, orange juice and lemon juice and stir well. Fill the pitcher with ice cubes. *As supplied by Dorothy and Sharlyn Davis.*

WHISKEY SOUR

serves 1

1½ tablespoons lemon juice
½ cup crushed ice
1 teaspoon powdered sugar
1 jigger (1½ ounces) bourbon whiskey

•

Combine the lemon juice and crushed ice in a cocktail shaker. Add the powdered sugar and bourbon, cover and shake well. Strain the mixture into a small glass and serve.

INDEX